Au Pair Guide

"If you don't travel,
you won't see anything."

John Letiane, Südafrika

Carmen Kurz

Au Pair Guide

A helpful handbook for your time abroad

With important information, addresses and numerous tips for everyday au pair situations, like dealing with children and common sicknesses, as well as an au pair dictionary

©2013 flyout Publisher House

Lohtorstr. 24, 74072 Heilbronn/Germany

Phone 0049 7131 5986768, Fax 0049 7131 5986769

info@flyout-verlag.de

www.flyout-verlag.de

ISBN 978-3-9814777-2-6

www.au-pair-guide.com

Au Pair Guide App is available in the App Store and Google Play Store.

Translated: John Dalbey

Cover design and layout: Kollmar Mediendesign

Typeset: Carmen Kurz

Photos: flyOUT archive and Fotolia

Contents

Foreword

Many young people have a desire to see the world after graduating high school. They want to experience something new before beginning their studies at college or starting their career.

As an au pair, you will live and work with a host family, supporting them with childcare and light housework. In return, you will earn some money while receiving free room and board. This provides you with an opportunity to experience another country and meet new people – becoming intimately and authentically familiar with their culture and language. It is a fascinating and exciting time, filled with new experiences and challenges that will give you a new perspective. Your host family is also looking forward to this intercultural exchange, which represents an important aspect of these programs.

During your stay with the host family, there will be some challenging moments. But these can also be very rewarding times if one is able to maintain a good attitude and perspective. This Au Pair Guide aims to help you get off to a good start and adjust to your new surroundings. It is your handbook for this new chapter of your life. Preparation, openness and an understanding for new cultures are the keys to a successful au pair experience.

But what is it like, living with a new family for a year? Or working with children? How does one handle a year without one's own family and friends? Can anyone apply for these programs? What requirements are there? What about language skills – how important are they? And what are the potential pitfalls?

In part I of the Au Pair Guide, you will find answers to many of these questions and receive a comprehensive overview of life as an au pair. Part II offers helpful information on how children develop and how to care for them. After all, these are the people you will be spending the majority of your time with. An overview of the most common child sicknesses and first aid tips are listed in part III. The detailed appendix also includes an au pair dictionary where you can find the most important terms and phrases in Spanish, French and German as well as a list of helpful web addresses.

Good luck and enjoy the read!

Carmen Kurz

Introduction

"I would love to spend a year in a foreign country, but I don't have much money!" I hear this all the time from people interested in hearing more about au pair programs. The au pair experience is different from other trips abroad. It is relatively inexpensive as the basic thought behind these programs is a balanced "give and take" approach. The term "au pair" is French for "reciprocity". The host family that takes you in and welcomes you into their family gives you the opportunity to experience the wonders of a foreign country, integrate into a new culture and make new friends along the way.

It sounds really simple, but leaving family and friends behind and adjusting to a new family marks the beginning of a new chapter in one's life. If you want to have a successful and enjoyable time abroad, you will need to be ready to try new things, leave familiar things behind and be open to change.

Preparing for Your Au Pair Experience

The preparations for your stay abroad as an au pair begin long before you leave home. It is best to start planning the basics of your trip about a year in advance. This time is used to mentally prepare for the upcoming trip. Think about what language you would like to learn and which countries you are interested in. Gather information on the culture, language, politics and history of your top 3 or so favorite countries. By familiarizing yourself with the history of a country, you will have a much easier time understanding certain traditions and customs. Consider how long you would like your stay to be. The longer your stay, the deeper and more familiar you will become with your host country's culture, language and overall lifestyle. Generally, an au pair program lasts for at least six months and most last a whole year. In the US, the guidelines are clearly defined and an au pair stay lasts at least 12 months. Other countries allow for shorter stays, such as a few months over the summer, but this depends on the respective country's entry requirements.

General Requirements

- Single and childless
- At least 18 years old
- Adequate language skills (sometimes only English skills are required – even in countries with different official languages)
- Valid ID and/or passport (validity should extend at least a few months beyond your planned return date)
- Physical and mental fitness
- Childcare experience
- Reliable and responsible character
- Clean criminal record certificate

Message from John:

An Au Pair in Germany
John from South Africa tells of his experience:

I can still remember it like it was yesterday: The dream of travelling to a foreign land. For me it didn't matter where it was – I just wanted to be out there, exploring the world and seeing how people live on the other side of the earth. The first time I heard about the au pair program in Germany, I jumped at the opportunity. I didn't even hesitate for a moment. I knew that this was my chance and I dove in head first.

Childcare experience can be gathered through internships at childcare facilities, babysitting work or tutoring as well as assisting or leading at a children's camp or sports center. This is a very important requirement, as childcare will be among your main tasks as an au pair and should not be overlooked. Your experience will need to be backed up with references. Practical experiences within your own family or references from relatives are generally inadequate.

Country-specific Requirements

Some countries have very specific requirements for au pair programs set by the government. For example, au pairs travelling to Australia or New Zealand need to show proof of sufficient finances for room and board and a return flight when entering the country. This assures the country that it will not have to financially support the incoming traveler. Australia also has a rule that limits an au pair to a maximum of six months per host family. Those wishing to stay longer have to switch to a new host family after six months. The US government stipulates that au pairs can only be placed by approved agencies. Private arrangements are therefore illegal in the US.

Depending on the host country, a visa may be required for entering and working in the country. Visa applications are only approved if one meets the host country's specific requirements. These can include the applicant's nationality, age, language skills, financial situation and health. This means that it may not be possible to be an au pair in your country of choice. The entry requirements and work provisions regarding your job as an au pair must be carefully followed. More specific information can be requested from the embassy of the respective country or an experienced au pair agency.

Points to consider: Language, country, length of stay, entry requirements

Tips & Tricks

The Traditional Au Pair Host Countries

Australia

Age	18–30
Language skills	Basic English
Working hours/week	Au pair 25–30 h, demi pair approx. 20 h plus 2 evenings of babysitting (au pair and demi pair)
Pocket money/week	Au pair AU$ 150–180 Demi pair approx. AU$ 80
Duration	6–12 months
Driver's license	Au pair: A driver's license is required Demi pair: Not required; left-hand traffic
Health insurance	Au pairs and demi pairs must take out an international health insurance policy.
Costs	Possible agency fees, travel costs for flights, visa fees, costs for international driver's license, international health insurance policy and AU$ 5,000 as reserve fund. The demi pair program costs about AU$ 5,000 for 3 months (incl. language school) plus travel costs, visa fees, insurance and reserve fund.

Special notes	You are limited to a maximum of six months with a family. It is possible to extend one's stay by switching to a new host family or by opting for a work & travel program. Both options are simple and straightforward.
Capital city	Canberra
Climate	Moderate in the south and east, while the north is tropical. Central Australia is desert.
Size	Approx. 7.7 million sq. km
Population	Approx. 22.5 million residents
Visa/entry requirements	Working holiday visa and work and holiday visa Further information is available from the Australian embassy
Official language	English
Currency	Australian Dollar (AU$)
Country code	+61
Emergency numbers	Police 000 Emergency medical services 000 Fire 000
National holiday	January 26 (Australia Day)

France

Age	18–26
Language skills	Upper intermediate level for Non-EU citizens in French. Basic French or good English skills for EU citizens
Working hours/week	Approx. 30 h plus 2 evenings of babysitting per week
Pocket money/week	At least € 60
Duration	6–12 months; short stays for au pairs from the EU can be arranged especially during summer.
Driver's license	Preferable, but not required
Health insurance	Host families have to register their au pair with the "URSSAF" – the French social security system.
Costs	Possible agency fees, travel costs
Special notes	Although host families are legally required to register their au pairs for social security, au pairs still have to take out additional private health insurance.
Capital city	Paris

Climate	Four major zones: Atlantic zone – moderate maritime climate; continental zone – marked temperature changes (especially in the east); Mediterranean zone – temperate warm maritime climate; alpine zone – harsh mountain climate.
Size	543,965 sq. km
Population	Approx. 64.3 million residents
Visa/entry requirements	No visa requirements for EU citizens. Further information can be obtained from the French Embassy.
Official language	French
Currency	Euro (€)
Country code	+33
Emergency numbers	Police 17 or 112 Emergency medical services 15 or 112 Fire 18 or 112
National holiday	July 14 (Fête nationale)

Germany

Age	18–26
Language skills	Basic German (level A1); for applicants from the EU, Australia, Israel, Japan, Canada, New Zealand and the USA a good command of English is sufficient, but basic German skills would be an advantage.
Working hours/week	Not more than 30 h plus 2 evenings of babysitting per week
Pocket money/week	At least € 65
Duration	6–12 months; short stays for au pairs from the EU can be arranged especially during summer.
Driver's license	Preferable, but not required
Health insurance	Host families must take out private health insurance for the au pair.
Costs	Travel costs, possible visa fees, possible agency fees
Special notes	Au pairs get two days of paid leave per month. Participation in a language course is obligatory. Au pairs have to pay for the course on their own.
Capital city	Berlin

Climate	Moderate oceanic/continental climate with frequent changes in weather
Size	357,021 sq. km
Population	Approx. 82 million residents
Visa/entry requirements	No visa requirements for EU citizens and for citizens from Australia, Israel, Japan, Canada, New Zealand and the USA. Further information can be obtained from the German Embassy.
Official language	German
Currency	Euro (€)
Country code	+49
Emergency numbers	Police 110 Emergency medical services 112 Fire 112
National holiday	October 3 (Reunification Day)

Great Britain

Age	18–27
Language skills	Basic English
Working hours/week	Approx. 30 h plus 2-evenings of babysitting per week
Pocket money/week	At least £ 70
Duration	6–24 months; occasionally some families are willing to host an au pair for 2-3 months during summer.
Driver's license	Preferable, but not required; left-hand traffic
Health insurance	Everybody can register with the National Health Service (NHS) free of charge or for a small fee. The NHS provides basic medical care. Taking out an additional private health insurance policy is therefore recommended. For further information see page 44.
Costs	Possible agency fees, travel costs, possible international insurance policy
Special notes	Many applicants choose Great Britain in order to learn "pure" British English. London and its surroundings is a very popular destination for au pairs. But there are many more places in Great Britain which are very interesting and not quite as multicultural.

Capital city	London
Climate	Moderate
Size	243,820 sq. km
Population	Approx. 62.2 million residents
Visa/entry requirements	The program is only open to citizens of the European Economic Area as well as for citizens from Australia, Canada, Japan, Monaco, New Zealand and Taiwan.
Official language	English, Welsh, Gaelic, Cornish
Currency	British Pound (£)
Country code	+44
Emergency numbers	Police 999 or 112 Emergency medical services 999 or 112 Fire 999 or 112
National holiday	Second Saturday in June (The Queen' s Official Birthday)

Ireland

Age	18–26
Language skills	Basic English
Working hours/week	Approx. 30 h plus 2 evenings of babysitting per week
Pocket money/week	€ 90–100
Duration	6–12 months; occasionally some families are willing to host an au pair for 2-3 months during summer.
Driver's license	Preferable, but not required
Health insurance	Au pairs must take out an international health insurance policy.
Costs	Possible agency fees, travel costs, international health insurance policy
Special notes	Irish Gaelic is only spoken in certain areas of the country. Most people, and especially the young generation, speak English.
Capital city	Dublin
Climate	Moderate ocean climate; mild winters, frequent changes in weather, heavy precipitation.

Size	70,282 sq. km
Population	Approx. 4.46 million residents
Visa/entry requirements	No visa requirements for EU citizens; Working Holiday Authorizations (WHA) are available to young people who are citizens of Argentina, Australia, Canada, Hong Kong, Japan, New Zealand, the US and the Republic of Korea.
Official language	English, Gaelic/Irish (3 %)
Currency	Euro (€)
Country code	+353
Emergency numbers	Police 999 or 112 Emergency medical services 999 or 112 Fire 999 or 112
National holiday	March 17 (St. Patrick's Day)

New Zealand

Age	18–30
Language skills	Basic English
Working hours/week	Au pair 30–40 h Demi pair approx. 20 h plus 2 evenings of babysitting per week (au pair and demi pair)
Pocket money/week	Au pair NZ$ 180–300 Demi pair NZ$ 60–80
Duration	6–12 months
Driver's license	Au pair: a driver's license is required Demi pair: not required, left-hand traffic
Health insurance	Au pairs und demi pairs must take out an international health insurance policy.
Costs	Possible agency fees, travel costs for flights, visa fees, costs for international driver's license, international health insurance policy and NZ$ 4200 as reserve fund. The demi pair program costs about NZ$ 3400 for 3 months (incl. language school) plus travel costs, visa fees, insurance and reserve fund.

Special notes	New Zealand is a special treat for nature lovers und sports enthusiasts. The unique landscape is great for sailing, hiking, skiing, surfing and many other activities. New Zealand has more sheep than people.
Capital city	Wellington
Climate	Moderate
Size	270,534 sq. km
Population	Approx. 4.35 million residents
Visa/entry requirements	Working holiday visa Further information is available from the New Zealand embassy
Official language	English and Maori
Currency	New Zealand Dollar (NZ$)
Country code	+64
Emergency numbers	Police111 Emergency medical services 111 Fire 111
National holiday	February 6 (Waitangi Day)

Spain

Age	18–26
Language skills	Knowledge of Spanish or English
Working hours/week	Approx. 30-33 h plus 2 evenings of babysitting per week
Pocket money/week	At least € 72
Duration	6–12 months; short stays can be arranged for applicants from the EU especially during summer.
Driver's license	Preferable, but not required
Health insurance	Au pairs must take out a private health insurance policy.
Costs	Travel costs, possible visa fees, possible agency fees, international health insurance policy
Special notes	Non-EU citizens must have proof of financial means to cover living expenses and a return flight home. For the completion of a full-time program leading to a degree or certificate, participants must be admitted into an authorized educational institution in Spain.
Capital city	Madrid

Climate	Madrid: highland climate (Castilian Plateau, 680 m above sea level), dry, cold winters, hot summers (up to 40 °C); coast: Mediterranean and Atlantic climate.
Size	505,990 sq. km
Population	Approx. 47 million residents
Visa/entry requirements	No visa requirements for EU citizens Further information is available from the Spanish embassy
Official language	Spanish (Castellano)
Currency	Euro (€)
Country code	+34
Emergency numbers	Police 112 Emergency medical services 112 Fire 112
National holiday	October 12

USA

Age	18–26
Language skills	Knowledge of English
Working hours/week	Up to 45 h
Pocket money/week	US$ 195.75
Duration	At least 12 months; it is possible to extend one's stay by 6, 9 or 12 months
Driver's license	A driver's license is required.
Health insurance	Health insurance will be provided by the host family.
Costs	Agency fees, visa fees, costs for international driver's license
Special notes	The host family pays for the flight and supports the au pair with up to US$ 500 tuition. Host families have to request au pairs through au pair agencies.
Capital city	Washington, D.C.
Climate	Generally moderate temperate zone
Size	9,826,630 sq. km

Population	Approx. 309 million residents
Visa/entry requirements	J-1 Visa More detailed information is available from the US embassy
Official language	English, in some places Spanish is also an advantage
Currency	United States Dollar (US$)
Country code	+1
Emergency numbers	Police 911 Emergency medical services 911 Fire 911
National holiday	July 4 (Independence Day)

Other Interesting Host Countries

Canada

Canada does not have an official au pair program. Those interested in a similar arrangement can apply for the "Live-in-Caregiver" program. This program is not limited to caring for children, but includes people of all ages. In order to successfully apply for a visa, applicants must be able to show 6 – 12 months of work experience as well as training in the nursing or care field. Those unable to fulfill these requirements can also enter the country on a working holiday visa. Applicants must be between 18 and 35 years old and have a clean background record. More information is available from the Canadian embassy. Sadly, the embassy only distributes a limited number of working holiday visas and these are only available for travelers of certain nationalities.

Scandinavia

The countries of Northern Europe are very popular thanks to their robust social systems. Scandinavian countries invest twice as much as other European countries into education and upbringing. This is a disadvantage for au pairs though. With their extensive national childcare systems, there are not many host families in need of an au pair in Scandinavia. Norway is unique with its social security requirements, which must be paid by the host family. In Iceland, on the other hand, host families cover the travel costs.

Of course there are other interesting host countries in Asia, Latin and South America. South Africa is also fairly popular as a host country. But since local personnel is usually much cheaper to come by in these countries than au pairs, who have to apply for visas and work permits, there are very few families interested in finding an au pair.

Message from John:

There were over 20 participants who were interested in the program and we had to take German lessons before we could apply for our visas. Only three of us stayed with it until the end. Some gave up because they had other work opportunities, some just bailed out without warning while others simply didn't show up to class. Learning German wasn't easy but I don't like to quit. For me, the hardest part was the waiting – waiting to find a family that would choose me as an au pair. My chances were already slim as a guy wanting to be an au pair. Even without issues of race, it is very difficult finding a family as a male. I also didn't have a driver's license, which didn't make things any easier...

Both my classmates found families before I did, which made me nervous. When a family chose me, I was overjoyed! The next step was scheduling a German test and applying for my visa. An A1-level German certificate is required as part of one's visa documents, so I had to work hard on the language side of things. All three of us passed the test. It isn't too difficult if you have good teachers and pay attention. Thankfully, we were well prepared. A lot of other paperwork was needed too, like a few passport photos, copies of the contract with the host family, a clearance and criminal record certificate, a doctor's test results for Hepatitis A, B and C, TB and HIV! All of these things cost money, which I didn't have. Thankfully, the organization running the project was willing to take on some of the fees. In total my visa cost me R2500.00 (about US$ 300)!

31

Au Pair or Demi Pair?

What is the difference? While an au pair works with the host family for the whole day, a demi pair only works for a half day – usually in the afternoons. During the mornings, a demi pair attends language school. The experience for a demi pair is a mix between a language trip and a work program. These are mainly offered in Australia and New Zealand and can last 3 to 6 months.

Since the language school adds an additional cost, the program is considerably more expensive than the usual au pair program. On the other hand, it is a great way to learn the language in a relatively short amount of time. At the end of the program, participants can receive a certificate, such as the Cambridge Certificate, TOEFL (Test of English as a Foreign Language) or IELTS (International English Language Testing System). These certificates represent a great advantage if one later chooses to apply at a foreign university or a job abroad.

The language school and the host family's house are usually located in close proximity to each other in larger cities. The schools are easily accessible using local public transportation and usually are close enough to walk to. An additional advantage is the intensive training at the language school and the diverse leisure program outside of school. Also in contrast to the au pair programs in Australia and New Zealand, the demi pair program does not require a driver's license.

Interested applicants that are not eligible for a working holiday visa due to their nationality can apply for the demi pair program on a student visa.

The Costs Associated with an Au Pair Program

Au pair programs are relatively affordable compared to other trips abroad. Room and board are provided by the host family and participants also receive a pocket money. Nevertheless, one must plan for expenses such as the following items:

- Agency fees, if an agency is used
- Travel costs
- Costs for a criminal record certificate
- Possible costs for international health insurance
- Costs for a language course either beforehand or during your stay in the host country
- Possible fees for a visa
- Possible fees for an international driver's license

Agencies charge a commission fee for their services. The extent of the fees is dependent on the host country selected and the services the agency provides. Additional fees for services such as support in applying for a visa, provision of telephone cards, international student IDs, insurance and preparatory seminars can also be charged. Upon arrival in the host country, there are introductory seminars, language courses and leisure activities that can also be booked for a price. Preparatory and introductory seminars are not absolutely necessary but can be very helpful in adapting to the new culture. It also provides you with an opportunity to make new friends right at the start of your trip.

USA The au pair program in the US is very different from other programs. While au pairs in other host countries have to cover the costs for travel to and from the country themselves, host families in the US assume these travel costs. Additionally, the host family supports the au pair with up to US$ 500 of tuition per year. In return, the au pair must commit to staying with the family for at least a full year.

Pocket money

As an au pair, you will receive a regular pocket money in the corresponding local currency. The size of the pocket money is set in accordance with the cost of living in the respective host country. You should bring some money for your first month in the host country, as the family is not required to pay your pocket money in advance and language courses generally require payment up front.

In some countries, the pocket money is paid to the au pair in cash at weekly intervals. This approach is straightforward and can save the au pair money on possible banking fees. Always get a receipt from the family to document the payments. In countries where debit cards are often used to make purchases, it makes sense to have the pocket money transferred to a bank account. Your host family can easily set up an automatic transfer order that will pay the money into your account regularly on a specific date. Before opening a bank account in your host country, it is recommended to compare the fees associated with maintaining an account at various banks.

Generally speaking, an au pair should be able to live from the pocket money they receive. However, you won't be able to afford any major splurges, so plan accordingly.

Finding a Host Family

Private Placement

"I found my host family through a friend of my mother," explains Lena, who sought advice from me due to problems with her host mother. Generally, there is nothing wrong with a private placement that locates a host family through recommendations from family, friends or relatives. On the other hand, if problems arise, it can make for a very uncomfortable situation. It can be especially difficult for the person who originally suggested the host family, as they often will be torn between the situations of two good friends or relatives.

Internet Platforms

Host families can also be found over so-called internet agencies. These are basically nothing more than platforms that provide short profiles on available host families and allow you to create your own profile. No advice, tips or other forms of support are offered here. Both sides get to know each other by viewing the respective profiles. No further information is available and the parties must enter an agreement on blind faith. Especially hasty invitations from host families should be assessed critically, with the pros and cons being weighed very thoroughly. If the host family is located in a major city and offering a very large pocket money, use extreme caution as these are the telltale signs of a scam.

"I quickly found a good au pair agency in my region. After submitting my documents, I received an online account that allowed me to view various host family applications."

Stephanie, au pair in US

Agencies

Advantages To prevent complications, it is recommended to make use of an au pair agency's services. They will advise you on how best to prepare, help you find a suitable host family, organize your departure and comply with quality standards. They are also a reliable contact during your stay abroad. Participants that have never left the country for an extended period of time and are nervous about the experience can discuss these fears and feelings with agency employees. Their experience allows them to offer solid advice and tips that help participants overcome their fears. Additionally, final exams, graduation parties and other obligations leave potential au pairs little time for planning and organizing their trip. These plans can be left to the agency. Agencies also give participants certificates upon completion of their trip. These are very beneficial when applying to a university or for a job. Private letters of completion, on the other hand, are generally not recognized.

Contact with Other Au Pairs Through the agency, you will also gain access to contact data for other au pairs. This allows you to get to know other participants around the world and make international friends. Additionally, the agency usually organizes events in the host country such as au pair meetings or trips. If there are no au pairs living in your host family's neighborhood, the agency will provide you with contact details of au pairs in the region for possible weekend visits or activities. You will never be able to travel as cheaply as you can as an au pair. In the US, every au pair is supported by a program coordinator. These coordinators organize events for au pairs in the region and are your point of contact should problems arise.

Compare Agencies To find the right agency, it is advisable to compare multiple offers. Important points to note are:

- Proven experience in au pair placement
- Good availability by telephone
- Membership in an association
- Support for visa applications
- Assistance for booking flights
- Insurance offers
- Provision of an international student ID
- Au pair workshops both at home and abroad
- Extensive consulting and informational material
- Commission fees
- Cancellation policies
- Support while abroad

Many agencies specialize in certain regions and have their focus either on European countries, the US or other foreign countries. Of course, there are also agencies that cover all of the usual au pair countries as well.

In general, agencies can be placed in one of two categories: private providers and non-profit organizations. The company type or its legal form is not a good indicator of quality – nor is its size. An agency that sends thousands of au pairs abroad is not any more or less likely to be better than one that sends only a few dozen each year.

A careful selection process that compares detailed information on the agencies is the best way to find the most suitable agency for your needs.

You can find a selection of agencies and request information from multiple organizations simultaneously by filling out a short search form at the following website:

www.au-pair-guide.de

Application Process

Every agency has its own application documents which they will send you on request. Usually there are helpful instructions on how to fill them out.

Documents
A complete au pair application generally includes the following components:
- Au pair survey
- Letter to future host family
- 1 passport photo
- Photos or a photo collage with pictures of the applicant
- Health certificate
- 1–2 childcare references
- 1–2 character references
- Clean background check
- Copy of school grades and/or work records
- Copy of passport
- Copy of driver's license, if applicable

The health certificate can be issued by your family doctor, who ideally is familiar with your health history. At the same time, you should ensure that your vaccinations are up to date.

"After sending my application documents off, everything moved pretty quickly. I had to go to an interview, which I was really nervous about – but it wasn't bad at all. Afterwards I received a few family profiles. The second family decided to take me right after the first telephone call."

Kyra, au pair in Australia

As soon as the documents have been received and checked by the agency, they are passed on to partner agencies in the target countries, which in turn pass the documents on to suitable host families. Many agencies maintain au pair galleries, which display a few photos and the basic data on each available au pair so that families can narrow down their search more quickly. Agencies are required to ask for your permission to display your photos and information in advance. Usually this permission is included as part of the agency's au pair application contract.

Many au pair applicants have special wishes regarding their host family, starting date, length of stay and location. An agency always does its best to satisfy these wishes. However, they cannot guarantee that every request will be 100 % fulfilled. One must keep in mind that the host families also have certain wishes and expectations as well. Even when a family has been found that meets all of your requirements, this does not necessarily mean that they will pick you as their au pair.

One of the most important questions that an applicant faces is: "How long will it take for a family to choose me?"

Placement Factors The probability of being chosen and the time it takes to be selected are highly dependent on the applicant's qualifications and certain placement criteria. Using the chart on the next page, you can get a rough idea of your placement prospects.

	Factors that could hinder your placement	Factors that can help a successful placement
Sex	Male	Female
Duration of stay	< 6 months	9–12 months
Age	18	> 19
Smoker	Yes	No
Driver's license	No	Yes and ample experience
Location of host family	Specific desires (city, region)	Flexible
Foreign language skills	None to very little	Good to very good
Childcare experience	None	Substantial experience
Piercing	Yes (piercings on the face are especially negative)	No piercings
Allergies / chronic diseases	Animal hair or food allergies; chronic diseases	Healthy with no allergies
Season of departure	Fall, since many applicants want to leave at this time	Spring or early summer
Boyfriend/Girlfriend	Yes	No

Applicants with more than 2 characteristics from the negative column should expect a longer wait. This does not mean that the applicant will not be placed. The time it takes to be placed is very dependent on which target country is chosen. For smokers, placement is generally very difficult. The same holds true for applicants without a driver's license in countries with lower population densities and/or countries with a poor public transportation infrastructure (USA, Australia, New Zealand).The second column represents the host families' most common preferences. An au pair does not have to fulfill all of a host family's preferences. The most important factor is the au pairs ability and willingness to adjust to the host family's needs. The same of course is true for the host family as well.

If a family is interested in your application, you will receive the family's application. This usually includes a family survey, a letter to you and a few photos of the family. If both parties are interested, communication via e-mail, telephone or Skype is then arranged.

Telephone Interview

A successful telephone interview requires some preparation. Very few families will call spontaneously without warning. Most will offer you the chance to set a date and time for the call. Remember that depending on the host country, there may be a significant time difference which will limit the possible times for a phone call. It is also therefore important to make sure that it is clear whose time zone is being used as the reference – the time in your home country or that of the host country – when setting the appointment.

Language Skills Applicants with good foreign language skills have a distinct advantage here. If you just recently graduated from a school where you learned a foreign language, communication shouldn't be a problem. If you haven't used your foreign language skills recently, you may want to refresh them by taking a short language course. Online language courses are becoming increasingly popular with people that work, as one can set one's own schedule for learning. Some of these courses are even offered for free, but they do require a great deal of self-discipline as there is no one pushing you to finish your homework. Your language skills will also play a major role during your first few weeks in the host country. The time difference and jet lag can be exhausting and there is lots of information to digest upon arrival. This requires a great deal of concentration and energy, especially if one is not completely fluent in the language. Preparation and practice are therefore highly recommended.

Questions from the Host Family These and similar questions are often asked by the host family during a telephone interview:

- Why would you like to be an au pair in a foreign country?
- Why did you choose this country?
- Have you ever been away from home for an extended period of time? Was it in a foreign country?
- What would you like to do during your stay here as an au pair?
- Do you have experience with children?
- How much experience do you have in managing a household?
- What are your responsibilities at home?
- Do you have any siblings? If so, how old are they?
- Do you have a driver's license and for how long? How much driving experience do you have?
- What are your hobbies?
- What do you do in your free time? Do you play any sports?
- Do you have a boyfriend/girlfriend?
- How would you describe your personality?
- Where did you grow up?
- How long have you been learning the language?

"I think one can enjoy any country if the host family is a good fit."

Nina, au pair in the UK and New Zealand

41

Questions to Ask the Host Family These are questions that are often asked by au pairs:

- In which city/region do you live?
- What is the closest major city?
- What are your hobbies and interests?
- What is your occupation?
- Are there other au pairs in your area?
- How many children do you have? Boys or girls? How old are the children?
- What tasks will I be responsible for as au pair? What will the average day look like?
- What do the children like to eat? What are their favorite meals?
- Do you have any pets? Will I be responsible for caring for them in any way?
- Do you live in a house or an apartment? Do you have a yard?
- How big is the au pair room? Do I have my own bathroom?
- Have you ever hosted an au pair before? Are you currently hosting an au pair? Would it be possible to contact the current au pair?
- How long would my working week be? How does this breakdown between the various tasks and days?
- How much of an pocket money would I receive?
- What recreational/entertainment possibilities will I have? How many vacation days will be available?
- Where is the nearest language school located?

These, of course, are only examples. Some of these questions will already be answered by the family's application documents. In any case, your first question should not be: "Where is the nearest language school and how often can I visit it?" If this question is what most interests you, you should probably consider a language trip rather than an au pair program. Questions on pocket money and vacation should also not be the focus of the conversation.

After the interview, everyone has time to consider whether this combination of au pair and host family is a good fit for both sides. When both sides give positive responses to the agency, the host family will make a formal invitation.

On the website for the British Broadcasting Corporation (BBC), there is a free program for learning English as well as current news from around the world.

http://www.bbc.co.uk/worldservice/learningenglish/ index.shtml

Online courses for other languages http://www.bbc.co.uk/languages

Maintaining Contact You should keep in regular contact with the host family all the way up until your departure. It is good for them to know that you are looking forward to meeting them in person and are already full of anticipation. Make sure to show your interest in the children as well as part of your communication with the family. Send them greetings or a few comments occasionally. This helps you set a foundation for the relationship before getting to know them personally.

"I was introduced to two families. I didn't like the first one which made the second one my choice. Since I suffer from a chronic illness, the agency told me that it may take longer to find a suitable family. But I was placed with a family after just one and a half months. It went much quicker than I expected!"

Stephan, au pair in the UK

To Do List

- First read this book and think about whether an au pair program really is the right choice for you

- If so, start collecting childcare references as soon as possible

- Learn more about the host countries that interest you

- Request informational material from various agencies and compare their prices and services

- Make a decision regarding the country you would like to live in, the length of your stay, which agency you will use and/or correct any previous decisions that have proven to be incorrect/not applicable

- Check the validity of your passport and IDs – make sure that the date of expiration is at least a few months beyond your planned return

- Prepare your application documents and turn them in to the agency of your choice

Now you have completed the first steps towards becoming an au pair and your agency will organize the next steps.

Insurance Abroad

Health Insurance
In some countries, the host family is legally required to set up a health insurance policy for the au pair. This includes countries like Germany, France, Norway, Iceland, the US and a few cantons in Switzerland. In

all other countries, the au pair is required to pay for th
insurance. The one exception here is the UK. There, th
system allows au pairs to simply register for health in
plans are even free. Sadly, medical care in the UK is not alwu,
best. Since the system provides care for free or for very low fees, one
can expect hefty additional fees or insufficient therapy services. Those
wanting to avoid nasty surprises in emergency situations should get an
additional international health insurance policy that covers medically
required return transport. This is generally not included in basic health
insurance policies.

Accident and Liability Coverage

Alongside of health insurance, accident and liability insurance provide
good all-around coverage. If you are covered by a family insurance policy
through your parents, you should check to see if the policy coverage
applies in the host country.

There are insurance companies that offer special policies custom-
tailored to au pairs. These know from experience what needs an au pair
has and offer a corresponding package of health, accident and liability
insurance and more.

The following provider offers global insurance for au pairs:
www.aupair-insurance-worldwide.com

Departure

Visa Once all of the formalities have been taken care of, it is time to
plan and prepare for your departure and entry into the host country. As
previously mentioned, some countries require a visa for entry.

When applying for a visa for the US or Europe, you must appear in person at an embassy or consulate. Applying for visas for Australia or New Zealand can be done using an online form. You can receive more detailed information from your placement agency or from the country's embassy directly. The costs for a visa vary from country to country, ranging between US$ 100 and US$ 280 in the usual au pair countries.

Planes or Trains? At the same time, you should be making your travel plans. What is cheaper: Travelling by train or with a plane? And more importantly, which is more practical? How close is your host family to an airport or train station? These things need to be sorted out with the host family. The same is true for your date of departure and arrival time. Make sure that the host family has time to prepare for your arrival and is up-to-date on all the details. If you are organizing the trip on your own, the simplest choice is usually to book a one-way flight with a low-cost airline.

Long-distance flights with a flexible return date are best booked through a travel agency.

"I met many au pairs on the flight to New York. We spent the first few days at a hostel and learned the agency's rules at a workshop. The week flew by and I could hardly wait to meet my host family."

Mareike, au pair in the US

Some agencies also offer to plan and organize travel for your trip. This is especially common when being placed in the US, since the host family is responsible for paying for your flight. Some agencies include services for booking the flight and transfer from the airport to a hotel or introductory seminar – particularly for trips to the US, Australia or New Zealand. If you are not participating in an introductory seminar, the host family will pick you up directly from the airport.

Message from John:

After all the visa requirements were met, a ticket could finally be booked for me. I was so nervous once I heard that the ticket to Germany had been bought. I had never flown before. In fact, I had never traveled outside of South Africa! I didn't know what it was going to be like, but I was too curious to be scared. The ticket cost R9777.00 (about US$ 1150)! Again this was money I definitely didn't have. Thankfully I could make arrangements with the organization that ran the au pair program. They paid for my ticket and I had to pay them back from my pocket money during my year abroad. I was just glad to have that behind me. Now all that was left to do was pack and say my goodbyes, which also wasn't easy. I was excited about the adventures ahead of me, but also sad to leave everything and everyone behind. The realization that I was leaving friends and family behind only really hit me once the plane's engines started. That was when I knew: This is it, I am going away now. It was a little scary as I didn't know what awaited me.

Packing Your Bags

In order to avoid bringing unnecessary items on your trip and possibly paying fees for extra baggage, it is wise to check the host country's climate in advance and select your clothing accordingly.

Here is a short checklist for orientation:

Carry-on Luggage

- Flight ticket/rail pass
- Host family's address and telephone number
- Contact data for the agency at home and abroad
- Cell phone
- Valid IDs and visa (if applicable)
- Proof of financial means (if applicable)
- Dictionary
- International driver's license
- Debit card, credit card
- International student ID
- Passport photos
- Copy of your vaccination card
- Proof of health insurance
- Some cash and a small currency conversion table
- Hygiene wipes and a travel toothbrush for long distance flights

Clothing

The general rule here is to not over pack. Like most au pairs, you will probably buy new clothes while abroad. Please keep in mind that you only have so much space in your bags for clothes. Often, au pairs realize shortly before their trip home that they don't have enough luggage space to take everything with them. If your host family has previously hosted au pairs, there is a good chance that they have a collection of things left behind.

"When packing, it's easy to think that you need to bring everything, but it isn't true. You'll end up buying a lot of things in the host country."

Senna, au pair in the UK

Leisure Items

- Travel guide (also available as an app)
- Digital camera or cell phone
- Notebook and pens
- Small laptop
- Photos from home
- Address book

Other Useful Items

- Adapter for electronic devices
- Important medications
- Gifts for the host family
- A replacement pair of glasses (if applicable)
- Charging cable for cell phone
- Small travel first aid kit (band-aids, ointments, cold sore cream, cough drops)

Gifts for the Host Family An object related to your home country always makes for a nice gift. This could be some kind of traditional handicraft, decoration or calendar with pictures of your homeland. Other potential gifts include wines, sweets, coffee or teas.

Good gifts for children include t-shirts, craft sets, toys, puzzles or a children's book from a popular children's author. For older children, sport merchandise, board games and outdoor games are ideal. The last type of game is especially good for breaking the ice during the first days.

On the day of your departure, you should remember to unplug all electronic devices in your room. The devices will use electricity in stand-by mode if left plugged in.

Make a copy of all of your important documents, such as your IDs, passport and bank cards as well as contact and travel data or scan them and save them as an attachment in an e-mail to yourself. These copies will come in handy should you lose an important document during your travels. Your agency will also have copies of some of your documents as they were included in your application.

Saying Goodbye Finally, the time has come to say goodbye to your family and friends at home.

Make sure to comply with all of the regulations regarding carry-on luggage at the airport. You are not allowed to carry containers with more than 100 ml of liquid for example. This includes items like deodorant, toothpaste, sprays and gels. Sharp objects like knives, scissors and nail clippers are also not allowed in carry-on luggage. Different airlines can have different rules for carry-on luggage, so be sure to check their policies before finishing your packing.

"I didn't spend my last night at home, because I didn't want to see my parents crying. The day of my departure was a blur. I guess I didn't want to believe that I was saying goodbye for almost a full year."

Nadine, au pair in Ireland

Arrival

First Contact After months of waiting and preparation, you finally arrive in the host country. The memory of meeting your host family for the first time at the airport or train station will stay with you forever. Perhaps they will stand there as a family greeting committee with colorfully drawn signs welcoming you into their country. Sometimes it is just one parent picking you up on their way home from work. This is usually dependent on your arrival time and your host family's schedule. Since you are still more or less strangers meeting for the first time, don't expect everyone to welcome you into the family with wide open arms. In particular, young children can be shy and it can take some time for them to open up to new people.

Message from John:

When I arrived in Germany, I had some problems finding my luggage. I had never been in an airport this big and I didn't know where to go or what to look for. It took a while before I found my bags. I actually found my family before I found my luggage. They were all waiting for me at the gate and somehow I appeared behind them. I still don't know how that happened. I was warmly welcomed by Tanja the mother, Frank the father and their little girl Analena, who I would be caring for and spending most of my time with over the next year. Having safely arrived in Germany, this was my new family now.

Your Temporary New Home Generally the first thing your host family will do is show you your new home. It might be an apartment or a house, perhaps with a large yard or none at all. If you aren't tired and still have some energy after your travels, maybe you can convince the children to give you a tour.

Another important point on the agenda is letting your family back home know that you've arrived safe and sound. Ask your host family if you can use the phone to call home.

while, you will learn where everything is located and how everything works in this new household. Don't be afraid to ask questions – you'll be living here a long time after all.

How does the unusual shower head work? Where is the light switch in the dark? Where do they keep the extra toilet paper? Where are the trash bins and is there a sorting system? Where are drinks stored? Where is dirty laundry kept? Are shoes allowed to be worn in the house? These are just a few example questions.

You will probably still be pretty tired when you wake up the next morning. Sleeping in a new environment, on a new bed with different sheets in addition to all the excitement can make it difficult to sleep peacefully at first. Sometimes the local climate also plays a role and requires some getting used to. Despite all of this, your host family will explain your schedule and role in the family, letting you know what is expected of you.

Important Items for the Start Your host family surely thought about how they can support you during your transition into this new phase of life. Here is a short list of items that are helpful when getting started:

- House key
- Map of the local area
- Dictionary
- SIM card and cell phone for local calls
- Bus or train timetables
- Notebook and pencil/pen

The Au Pair Guide app contains additional tips on life as an au pair as well as cheap travel ideas and assistance on finding the right language course in your host country. Available in the App Store and Google Play Store.

Tips & Tricks

Important Contact Data

Make a list of important telephone numbers and addresses that you can easily find in an emergency. You should learn some telephone numbers by heart, such as those for the police, fire department and emergency medical services. Hanging the list in your room can be helpful for memorizing these telephone numbers.

You can use the following example contact list as a guide for the one you create with your host family:

Phone number and postal address of the host family

Host Mother	Host Father
Mobile	Mobile
Work	Work
Grandparents	
Further relatives	
Friends	
School/Kindergarten	
Police	Fire Service
Ambulance	Family Doctor
Pediatrician	Au Pair Agency

You as Au Pair

A key to having a successful au pair experience is going into the job with the right expectations. As an au pair, you will undoubtedly have an opportunity to dive into a new culture. It could be that your host family lives in the climate of your dreams or is located at the heart of a major city that never sleeps. As incredible as this can be, you should never forget that an au pair trip is not a vacation. Your main task is caring for the host family's children. This work can be pretty challenging at times as every family and every child is different from others. Each has their own individual needs and sometimes it is difficult for them to even put these needs into words.

Most au pairs are very busy during their first few weeks with the host family. There is a lot to learn and it requires your full attention. Since communication in a foreign language can be tricky at times, observation plays a key role. If something is unclear, you should always ask for clarification. Many things will be done differently here than they would be back home. That is why it is all the more important that you remain open to this other mindset and accept this new lifestyle.

What Is Expected of You as an Au Pair

The ideal au pair pleases both young and old alike. The host family decided to invite you into their family and therefore declared themselves willing to assume the costs for your stay (room & board, etc.). In return, they expect that you not only fulfill the basic legal requirements for being an au pair, but that you also bring the necessary personal competencies and attitude for the job.

Respect

The golden rule is international: Treat others as you would like to be treated. You are expected to treat your host family with the same respect and dignity that you would have for your own parents.

Care

The family will ask you to carry out certain tasks. Perform these tasks with care and attention to detail. Treat the host family's property even better than you would your own. In return, you will receive the family's recognition and financial reimbursement in the form of an allowance. Both of these rewards should motivate you to do the best job you possibly can. Recognition and appreciation from the host family will help you feel part of the family. You reflect that appreciation by doing a good job.

Flexibility

Just about everything is new and different in the beginning. The host family, the new culture and lifestyle, the climate and new time zone all take some time to get used to. In order to have the best possible transition, you need to be mentally and emotionally prepared to take on these challenges. Your host family will expect you to adjust fairly quickly. Many things will seem strange to you, but it is important that you stay open minded and not be too hasty to judge. Keep a positive outlook and try to find the good in everything – even the things that seem completely backwards to you.

Caring for the Children

Most families choose an au pair as a type of older sibling for their children – someone who will establish a personal relationship with them. Au pairs offer greater flexibility than a daycare and can watch the children at home.

Every host family wants their children to be tended to with love and care. That's why it is so important that you have some previous experience in childcare before starting your au pair program. If you have trouble getting along with children, are impatient by nature or are quickly stressed out by unexpected situations, you probably shouldn't apply for an au pair program.

Personal Criteria In addition to the general requirements that an au pair should fulfill, the following personal characteristics are also highly recommended for a successful au pair experience:

- Good general education
- Interest in expanding your foreign language skills
- Maturity
- Enthusiasm
- Flexibility
- Interest in the host country and host family

What You Can Expect from Your Host Family

- A host family consists of parents, married or single, with children under the age of 18
- Appreciation and respect
- Inclusion into the family: e.g. eating with the family and joining them on family trips and excursions
- A daily or weekly plan with a list of your tasks and responsibilities
- Pocket money, which is agreed on in writing
- Contractually set weekly working hours
- The opportunity to visit a language course
- At least one full day off per week
- A set amount of vacation
- Your own room

Your Room The room where you will live during your time as an au pair with the host family should come with its own lock, be neat and tidy on the day of your arrival and have a window. It should also have a bed, a closet, a table and a chair. They are not required to provide you with your own bathroom however.

The Tasks of an Au Pair

The tasks of an au pair generally fall under two categories: childcare and light housework. The au pair is not completely responsible for these tasks, but rather is meant to support the parents in these areas and lighten their load.

1. Childcare

Childcare means that you as an au pair are jointly responsible for the children's everyday needs. This includes for instance:

Entertainment and Supervision Playing with the kids, bringing them to kindergarten, school, leisure events or play dates with friends, reading to them, doing crafts with them, exercising with them, helping them with homework, etc.

Feeding Preparing small meals or snacks, serving the food

Physical Hygiene Washing and bathing the children, brushing their teeth, changing their clothes

Bathroom-related Duties Changing diapers, assisting small children in the restroom, potty training

Sleeping Waking the children in the morning, bringing them to bed at night, laying them down for a nap

Safety Supervising the children and keeping them from danger, taking them by the hand when crossing the street, never leaving small children unsupervised

2. Light Housework

The second main task alongside of childcare is helping around the house. This can include the following tasks:

- Tidying up
- Washing clothes and ironing
- Vacuuming
- Airing the house
- Dusting
- Mopping
- Caring for pets (dogs, cats, guinea pigs, etc.)
- Going shopping
- Preparing and serving small meals or snacks
- Cleaning up the kitchen
- Washing dishes
- Looking after the house/apartment when the family is away

Occasionally there is need for some discussion between the au pair and the host family on what qualifies as light housework. Generally, light housework consists of the normal everyday tasks that need to be tended to in the household.

A Typical Day for an Au Pair

What does the average day look like for an au pair?
Here is an example day in a host family with two children (Sam, 3 years old, and Meghan, 7 years old):

7:00 am Wake up.
8:00 am Help prepare breakfast for Sam and Meghan.
  ➢ *Observe the children during the meal. Ensure that they are clean and properly clothed for the day's weather.*
Accompany Meghan to school and Sam to kindergarten. Once back

home, make the beds and clean up the breakfast table. If necessary vacuum, tidy up, do laundry or iron.

1:00 pm Pick up Sam from kindergarten and have lunch together. Play together afterwards until it's time for his nap.

> ➤ *While he is sleeping you can read, relax, etc. Just do not leave the house!*

After his nap, you can go to the playground together or play in the backyard.

> ➤ *If something basic needs to be bought at the store, like bread, you can take the children on a short shopping trip.*

3:30 pm Meghan comes home from school and will be hungry.

> ➤ *Prepare a small snack (fruits).*

Sam and Meghan can play together, but Meghan must also finish her homework...

> ➤ *...and you will need to ensure that she does it.*

5:30 pm Parents return from work.

6:30 pm Get the kids ready for dinner (wash hands). Dinner.

8:00 pm Language course.

For you as an au pair, it is important that you adapt to the family's work/life rhythm. Your working hours are generally spread over the day. In the example above, you have about 1.5 hours of work in the morning and 4.5 hours in the afternoon.

"The first time I went to pick up my host family's little boy from school, they thought I might be a kidnapper. My host family got a call saying that a stranger had come to pick up Josh from school."

Jan, au pair in Australia

59

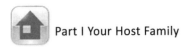

Your Host Family

A family is a close-knit group with many shared experiences over the years. As an au pair, you suddenly join this group as a new member. Everyone has to adjust to this new situation.

The relationship between the au pair and the host family develops quickly and this isn't always an easy and comfortable transition. After all, a family builds relationships with its other members over years. Please keep in mind that every family is different. Try not to compare your host family with other host families or your family back home. No family is the same. Every family comes with their own unique set of "plusses and minuses". The fact that your host family allows you into its private life is a sign of its trust in you. You should view this as a rare privilege or gift that the family is offering you.

Ethnic Background of the Host Family

In countries with a high immigration rate, some host families will not have the same nationality as the host country. Or their ancestors may originally be from another country, which might be recognizable from their skin color, last name or religion for instance. Openness for different ethnic groups is a requirement for a successful time abroad.

Remember that when you go abroad, you too are a foreigner.

Rules and Guidelines in the Host Family

Every family has its own rules and guidelines. They generally aren't written down or published anywhere, and yet they exist. Some rules are clearly and vocally expressed while others are communicated in a more subtle manner. You can recognize them in the general behavior of the various family members, how they comply with both spoken and unspoken rules. This means that you can learn most of a family's rules and guidelines simply by observing their behavior closely.

You should feel at home with your family. That's why it is important that you understand their rules. If something is unclear, you need to ask for clarification. This will help prevent possible misunderstandings or uncomfortable situations with the various members of the family.

You might find the following or similar rules being applied by your host family:

- Everyone comes to the breakfast table dressed and ready to start the day
- Meals are started and finished together
- Doors are locked at night
- Shopping is done only once per week
- Sleeping or eating is restricted to certain times of the day
- The TV is turned on only after 6 pm
- Laundry is done twice a week
- There is a schedule for who is allowed to use the bathroom, etc.

Got It? Check to see that you understand all of the rules. You will pick up many of the recurring processes or procedures without even realizing it. Minor misunderstandings often occur during the first few weeks where the language differences can represent a formidable hurdle. That's why it is recommended that you repeat your host family's rules or instructions in your own words so that both parties can be sure that you have understood the intended meaning of the message.

Job Schedule Ask your host family for a schedule that clearly lays out your tasks and responsibilities. It should list all of your tasks and how often you will need to do them. The plan is only meant as a guide for the initial adjustment phase. Later, you will be expected to handle certain tasks on your own. Everyday tasks that you know from family life at home, such as setting and clearing the table, emptying the dishwasher, taking the dog for a walk, watering the plants or collecting the mail should be easy to handle from day one.

Get to know the household's various devices (washing machine, microwave, etc.). Ask what devices and utensils will be needed for your tasks and if there is anything you are not allowed to use. Write down the instructions for using the devices so that you can use them without support the next time.

As previously stated, an open mind and good communication are very important. Understand that the host family will be the ones that define what the rules are. You need to respect and honor this. If something seems strange to you, ask for clarification. Surely there are reasons why your host family thinks certain things are right or wrong. As they say: When in Rome, do as the Romans do.

General Rules

1. Be punctual.

2. Inform your host family beforehand when you have plans to meet with friends.

3. Be careful with passing on contact information, especially concerning data from or about your host family.

4. Your attitude should never negatively impact the host family. Never talk to the neighbors about your host family's private life. Respect other people's privacy.

5. Vacations and leisure time should be planned in advance together with your host family.

6. Actively participate in your host family's activities, such as family meal times, social and cultural events and other family activities.

7. Keep your room neat and tidy. Also do your part to keep shared rooms like the bathroom, living room and kitchen clean.

8. Don't let any strangers into the house if you are alone.

9. Ask your host family if friends can visit you at home.

10. Let your host family know at what time you will be returning home whenever you leave the house. If you will return later than expected, it is advisable to call your host parents and inform them so that they don't stay up waiting for you. If you return at a time where people are likely sleeping, try to be quiet so that you don't wake anyone.

11. If you are asked to watch the kids in the morning, make sure you don't stay up too late the night before. You should check out the local nightlife on days where you'll be free to sleep in the next day.

12. Only use the telephone, computer and internet for private use according to your arrangements with the host family.

13. If you have a boyfriend or girlfriend, only bring them home if you have permission from the host family in advance.

14. Don't cause any unnecessary costs for your host family by making frequent long-distance calls or breaking things around the house. They have the right to ask you for compensation for damages. You can find more information on telephone and internet use on page 69.

15. When driving with the children, be especially careful not to take any unnecessary risks. Observe all safety precautions during the drive for both you and the children (safety belt, child seat, glasses/contacts if needed, etc.).

16. If you spend the household's money on food or items for the children, save the receipts so that the family can see what you spent their money on.

Living with the Host Family

Every family is its own small world. Accepting a new person into this microcosm requires openness from all parties involved.

To make this transition as smooth as possible, it is wise to observe what behavior is deemed "normal" in the host family. It is also advisable to observe how the relationships between the individual family members are structured and how you fit in.

"In the beginning, I had to find out what kind of values my "new" family had and what they viewed as important. You have to find your place in the hierarchy so to speak without rocking the boat."

Nadine, au pair in Ireland

Since the host family assumes responsibility for the au pair and treats you like a member of the family, they also have the authority to make certain rules like normal parents would. Some of these rules may seem stricter than those you know from your family back home. This can be due in part to the different morals and values that certain countries have in comparison to others.

Sometimes host parents will not want to make any rules for you. They view you as an adult and not as their child. This makes your relationship more like that of friends rather than a child/parent relationship.

There are host families that want to completely integrate the au pair into their family life while others prefer an au pair that is independent and occasionally spends free time away from the family. Regardless of which type of host family you have, you should always try to develop your own friendships outside of the family during your stay.

Location

Not every host family lives in a major city and not every country has a high population density.

Naturally, cities offer more opportunities with regards to leisure activities and cultural events. On the other hand, it is generally easier to get to know local people in a more rural setting.

"I'm happy that my family doesn't live in the city. Today, I chased a lizard for a half an hour. I love to see animals and wildlife in their natural habitat rather than in a zoo. All I can say is: Australian nature is fascinating!"

Jan, au pair in Australia

Message from John:

I didn't experience too much culture shock when I arrived at the Impfingen district of Tauberbischofsheim (the city the family lived in). It was a very quiet but friendly neighborhood. Once the formalities of registering me at the City Hall and Registration Office were done, I was officially part of the neighborhood. I got to know the neighbors pretty quickly as they all knew I was coming. The first few weeks were all about getting to know the family and their friends as well as learning how everything functioned and operated in the house. During this time, I was introduced to my duties and what was required of me. I learned them pretty quickly – the family was a good family and they were great teachers. Once I got the hang of things, I would be left every now and then to take care of the child and look after the house alone.

65

Working Hours and Free Time

The topic of working hours and free time is a common point of conflict between au pairs and host families, as the work requirements aren't as clearly defined as in other jobs. Activities like setting the table and cleaning up afterwards are a normal part of family life and generally aren't viewed as working time. Babysitting is also viewed similarly by some families.

Here is an example: Your host mother asks what you have planned for the evening. Since you have no specific plans, she asks you if you wouldn't mind watching the kids for the evening. She puts the kids to bed and you just have to be there in case a child wakes up and needs something. While you are babysitting, you can pass the time just about any way you like (watching TV, chatting, reading, etc.). This means that it isn't pure working time where every hour is counted. It is viewed merely as babysitting and is generally applied on a per evening basis towards your working hours. If you stay home every night, it is understandable that your host parents may eventually end up taking this for granted. You can avoid this scenario by occasionally spending evenings away from home. Usually this would mean meeting friends in town, going to a language course or involvement in some kind of sports team or club. If you simply decline to babysit because you feel like you're being taken advantage of, it can leave an uncooperative impression. The host parents will ask you: "Why can't you babysit if you're spending the evening at home anyway?"

In order to really enjoy your free time, you should occasionally leave the host family's apartment or house. A child cannot differentiate between working hours and free time and will want to play with you during all hours – including your free time.

Make sure you give your host family advance notice of your free time plans in order to avoid any scheduling conflicts. If differences of opinion cannot be avoided in this way, sometimes it helps to write up a schedule together that has the exact times and tasks that are expected and clearly shows when you are free to do as you like.

"I can't wait for the weekend! Chilling with friends in Sydney."
Jan, au pair in Australia.

Language

Verbal communication with your host family will sometimes be difficult. Talking about problems can be especially complicated. It is ok to occasionally remind your host family that you have some difficulties with the language. Don't be offended when they correct your pronunciation as native speakers of the language. They just want to help you in your efforts to learn the language. With time, your language skills will improve. Some host families are also interested in learning the au pair's native language. This leads to mutual learning and teaching.

Message from John:

The family was very busy and traveled a lot. They needed someone to take care of their child occasionally. I was quite a hit with the kids in the neighborhood and everybody knew me. It was almost impossible NOT to know me, as I was practically the only au pair and African guy around.

It wasn't easy communicating entirely in German, but I soon realized that I had no other choice as it's the only official language in Germany. My host family was very supportive in helping me learn their language and „culture".

Everything was strange and new: the people, the sights and even the smells. These new experiences helped me realize that I was no longer in South Africa.

67

Language Courses

Most au pairs participate in a language course one to two times a week. Au pairs generally have to pay for the language course on their own. Your schedule for the language course will be dependent on your host family's working hours. This should be worked out with your host family before you sign up for any courses. If there isn't a language school located near your host family, it can sometimes be helpful to arrange for an intensive language course in a bigger city during your vacation time. Another option would be to take a language course before starting your au pair trip. Again, as with the other possibilities, you will be responsible for covering the costs associated with the course.

Do not expect your host family to give you time off every day to visit a language course. This only applies to demi pairs.

Food

There are many new dishes and foods to try while abroad. Perhaps even breakfast is different than what you are used to back home. Whatever the case may be, don't expect your host family to make something different for you every day. You are expected to participate in the family meals and eat the same things they are eating. If food begins to become an issue, perhaps you can help arrange a meal plan with the host family and help when shopping for groceries, or maybe even do the shopping yourself. This gives you an opportunity to see what new foods are out there and allows you to influence what will be on the menu. Many families prefer fresh foods to fast food. Whatever their preferences, you need to accept them! Your host family would also likely be more than happy to try a traditional dish from your native land.

Religion

Religion is a part of culture and can influence the behavior of a society in various ways. Your host family might have a different faith than you. Respect their religion and they will respect yours in return.

Travel & Vacation

In most countries, an au pair stay lasts 12 months with 2 weeks of paid vacation. Sadly this isn't standard across the board, as these rules generally follow the work regulations of the specific country. Generally, you can only take vacation if you have received advance approval from your host family. After all, they often depend on your childcare services. Au pairs are often brought along on family vacations. Your tasks and responsibilities during the vacation should be discussed and determined before leaving on the trip. Otherwise it is possible that the host family will have a vacation while you work, and yet the days will count as vacation days for you.

Do you have plans to meet with friends and travel around? Even if you want to travel on your own, always inform your host family of your plans well in advance.

It is also a good idea to keep your host family informed during your trip, just to let them know that you are safe and everything is OK. Especially if you are travelling alone, it is a good idea to inform them of where you are and where you are headed next via e-mail or text message. Au pairs are regularly reported as missing because they get lost, take the wrong train or their cell phone battery dies. A quick message gives your host family peace of mind.

Telephone & Internet

Please do not use the host family's telephone for long conversations whenever possible. There may be friends or relatives trying to call and they may find it annoying when they can't get through. The family might also be unhappy if they find out you have been having long phone conversations during your working hours and possibly incurring costs for the family.

Frequent communication with family and friends back home can easily lead to homesickness.

Tips & Tricks

The internet has become a convenient and effective tool for communication and an integral part of everyday life. That's why you need to clarify the rules surrounding computer and internet usage with your host family at an early stage. Be careful when downloading files from the internet! Everything you do on the internet can be traced back to the computer you used, which includes any illegal activities or purchases you make online, so be responsible. Also be careful with contact details and private information regarding your host family. Don't post embarrassing stories about the host family on Facebook or announce to the world that the house will be empty for two weeks while everyone goes on vacation.

Get a local SIM card for your cell phone in order to avoid roaming costs. Check to make sure your phone will work in the host country if you plan on using your cell phone from back home. Not all phones work in all locations, so be sure to check in advance. Skype is a great tool for making international calls or even video conferencing with family and friends back home. You can download the program for free at www.skype.com.

Tips & Tricks

Turn Off Your Cell Phone Surfing the web while watching the children is irresponsible. Please concentrate on the kids when you're in charge of supervising them. Surfing the web and making phone calls are free time activities. Both can distract you from watching the children and they will often use those moments to get into trouble.

"I now know what I will do differently when I have my own children."

Katharina, au pair in the UK

Complications

Sometimes there will be moments where things are not going as well as you had hoped. Everyone has a bad day occasionally. Sometimes it helps just to talk with someone about how you are feeling. Even just writing them down in a diary can be helpful. The worst thing you can do is bottle everything up inside as this often leads to a feeling of loneliness. Try to avoid this by making contact with other au pairs.

Conflicts with the Host Parents

It may be that you are not the au pair that your host family had hoped for. It could also be that your host family isn't what you were hoping for. In such cases, both sides have to make certain compromises and be open to new perspectives. Patience and understanding are important here. Differences must be respected. Be courageous and don't respond with a full blown retreat. It is exactly in these difficult moments that you need to try to talk it out with your host family.

> Don't judge the host parents for how they raise their children.

Talking About Difficulties If you have the feeling that your host family is asking too much of you, set up a meeting with them where you can talk. Preferably somewhere quiet where the conversation will be undisturbed. It can sometimes be helpful to jot down some notes about what exactly is bothering you, so that you have the words and examples with you in case you forget. You can also talk to an employee at the agency if you are having problems. They can often give you good tips based on their experience.

"Everything has three sides: One that you see, one that I see and one that we both can't see."

Chinese proverb

Message from John:

I had my ups and downs with the family – usually the problems stemmed from a communication breakdown or failure. I heard from other au pairs that this is common. The family would say one thing and I would understand another, or I would try to do things my way and it wouldn't fit that well in the family's view. But whatever issues we had, we could always talk about them. I had my mistakes and they had theirs. Sometimes it was a matter of one side pushing for what it believes is right and the other fighting for their say. I don't easily back down from an argument and it's hard for me to change my mind once I am convinced of something. This was occasionally a setback for our communication.

In cases where the host family is truly exploiting you, the best choice is usually to end the au pair relationship.

Before assuming the worst, however, be sure to consider that working conditions vary from country to country and are usually reflected in the au pair program. While au pairs in Germany work a maximum of 6 hours per day and a maximum of 30 hours per week with 2 days of paid vacation per month, au pairs in other countries can sometimes work 8-10 hours per day with only 1 unpaid vacation day per month. Be sure to know what applies to your situation before signing up!

Important: If your host parents criticize you, please do not take it personally or be offended. Most likely they just want to show you a particular problem and help you improve.

Conflicts with the Children

Unfortunately, sometimes the child or children can be a source of frustration as well. You need to be prepared for such scenarios. Ask your host parents for tips on how they deal with their child or children in difficult situations. Perhaps you can ask to observe the child at school and see how the teachers and other children interact with your host child. Children often test authority. They want to know how far they can go and where the limits are. That's why it is important to be aware of what rules apply to the child and have a plan for enforcing them. Be consistent. The parents will ultimately decide what the child is allowed or not allowed to do. Never use violence to convey your disapproval with a child.

Parents love their children and are happy when they hear a positive report about them. That's why a critical discussion can sometimes be difficult. Don't be scared, but express your understanding and tolerance as part of the conversation. Even if a misunderstanding occurs, this is a chance for you to work on your communication and diplomatic skills. Generally, misunderstandings and problems can be worked out if you really do your best to stay patient and objective. If this isn't possible, read the section on ending the au pair relationship.

Ending the Au Pair Relationship

If the problems you are experiencing with your host family cannot be solved, it is usually best to move to a new host family. The first step is informing the agency of your situation. Your au pair contract comes with a cancellation period that will need to be observed. This is usually 14 days, unless something has occurred which calls for an immediate termination. This period can be especially difficult since both parties are usually unhappy with the situation and may have some built up aggression. It can however be a positive time, as both parties also can now see light at the end of the tunnel and know that a new start is coming. Usually both sides want a peaceful separation. If you have leftover vacation, you can subtract this from the cancellation period.

With a mutually desired separation, the cancellation period is not as important. It basically allows the host family to find another solution and gives you time to talk with the agency about finding a more suitable host family. Remember that your host family has no right to keep you from leaving. You are a free individual and are free to make your own decisions.

"Unfortunately, problems began to arise shortly after joining my host family and we were unable to find a positive solution. This meant that I had to change families basically right at the start. This made me doubt whether I had made the right choice in coming to America. But having been through it, I can only recommend patience for those experiencing a similar situation. It truly is a once in a lifetime opportunity to experience the American Way of Life."

Mareike, au pair in the US

Think Positively

Always try to find the positives in negative situations. Failure and disappointments are also opportunities for a fresh start. Those able to stay motivated and positive when disappointments come have an advantage when facing difficult situations. Everyone experiences highs and lows in life. Getting out of the low periods requires the will to stand up and keep trying. The ability to control your emotions and remain objective in conflict situations is another important skill. You can only learn this by experiencing conflict situations and getting to know your own emotions. People that know how to manage their emotions have an advantage in nearly every area of life.

"It is worth remembering during the trip that you are always free to go home. No one HAS to stay and suffer through a bad situation. This thought helped me to not give up, but to try another host family instead. Being strong and patient really paid off in the end."

Kristin, au pair in Spain

Conflicts are a part of life and important for improving our social skills.

Culture Shock

As we grow up, we get used to a certain environment. We call this our culture. This culture influences our lives in various ways – it affects our thinking, emotions and behavior. When we take a trip abroad, many things are new to us and perhaps seem strange. With every experience we discover something new. On a vacation, this adventurous lifestyle can be a lot of fun. But when we try to live our everyday life in a strange, new place for an extended period of time, it can make us uncertain and insecure, which in turn can lead to failures and frustration. Everything seems different. People from different cultures react to certain situations differently and also perceive things differently. This can easily lead to misunderstandings and if these reoccur often enough, it can become a psychological burden. We generally call this "culture shock".

Culture shock generally doesn't start at the beginning of your trip. The first few days or weeks are usually filled with the euphoria of being on a new adventure. The walk through the park is fascinating and shopping in the supermarket is suddenly far more exciting than it ever was back home. The host family takes their time to help you adapt and settle in, showing lots of patience and understanding. You make new friends and are happy – just like a vacation. But as soon as the daily routine sets in, you begin to realize that this is very different from a vacation. The host family has less time now, since they have to catch up on various private and professional obligations. The hospitable consideration you received in the beginning starts to transform into normal family life. Some of the au pairs you've met in the area go back home. Others don't have as much free time now or have developed other interests. The search for a perfect language course is proving to be harder than expected and constructive criticism is sometimes misinterpreted as a personal attack. Frustration and dejection began to cloud your emotions.

The following symptoms can arise from culture shock, though their duration and intensity can vary from person to person:

- An aversion towards the host country, its language and culture
- A strong desire for your native language, home culture and familiar food
- Irritability, aggressiveness
- Eating disorders such as loss of appetite or compulsive eating
- Depression, tiredness
- A strong conviction that your culture is superior to the other

"After 3 months, I experienced my first funk. I was beginning to be critical of nearly everything and missed some typical German things. But thankfully I was able to overcome it pretty quickly."

Katharina, au pair in the UK

Message from John:

Sometimes I felt alone and thought nobody understood me. And I was right: Nobody understood me. Nobody was experiencing what I was experiencing. I was in a foreign land, with no friends or family who spoke my language or understood my beliefs and opinions. I had friends in Germany that I knew from South Africa and I had also contact to the au pair agency for help when I needed it. But this feeling of isolation was very difficult for me to get over. Carmen, a staff member at the agency, told me how German families value their kids and how they can be adamant on how their children are raised. She was the bridge between me and the family.

I also had lots of fun and good times with the family. They invited me to almost every function they attended and took me to see theme parks as well as some of the neighboring countries (Switzerland, Czech Republic and Denmark). They also made sure I was out having fun and making friends. I got to know a few au pairs from the neighboring villages and towns. We met every now and then and talked about our experiences. This helped a lot, as these people knew exactly what I was going through. They were having the same issues and were in the same situations that I was in. We had a lot in common and it really helped to talk together. And it wasn't just our work that we discussed: We also talked about life itself and our plans for the future. While we may not have spoken the same native language, we understood each other when it came to life in Germany. I really recommend talking to other au pairs as this helps you see that you are not alone. There are many other au pairs going through similar situations from all over the world.

In order to get over this slump more quickly, you should try to view your new environment as objectively as possible. Actively try to meet new people and make contact with au pairs of different nationalities.

You will see that this problem doesn't just apply to you, but that au pairs from other cultures also have similar difficulties. Try to improve your language skills by getting to know some of the locals. This is a sign of your maturity and independence and will show you just how well you can make it on your own. This new group of friends will be your support system, helping you through the tough days. You can get to know local people your age at sport clubs or in youth organizations.

In Other Words: Get out there and experience your new home! This new place is not going to adapt to you – you will have to adapt to it, so take a deep breath and dive in!

Homesickness

You can be sure that this feeling will come at some point during your stay abroad. Practically everyone who is away from home in a foreign country for an extended period of time experiences homesickness. The symptoms and effects are similar to culture shock, but generally aren't as extreme. Especially on holidays such as Christmas, New Year's and Easter, one feel's drawn to family and friends back home. Host families often ask about the traditions in your home country during such holidays, which only amplifies the longing for home. Most au pairs become melancholy or sad when reporting about their traditions back home: the food, the religious background and family experiences. A phone call to family back home can often be helpful here as well as talking to other au pairs. Doing nothing or sitting around the house is definitely counterproductive as this only increases the feeling of loneliness and depression.

Try to decorate your room with personal objects and really make it your own space. But don't spend too much time there – get out and experience life in your host country!

Tips & Tricks

When the End Draws Near

The au pair experience seems to fly by. The date for your trip back home draws closer and closer and you should be planning your next steps for what you will do once you return home. As you think about everything you have experienced during your time in the host country, you will be overwhelmed with a mix of emotions. On the one hand you will be happy to see your family and friends back home again. On the other, you will have to leave your host family, which has become your second home. You will have to say goodbye to all the friends you've made in the host country. It can be a painful goodbye – not knowing if or when you will see these people again. Comfort yourself with the many personal enrichments that you have gained during your invaluable time abroad.

Goodbye Gifts Your host family deserves a special thank you at the end of your stay. They accompanied you throughout your time abroad, teaching you new things and giving you the opportunity to participate in the au pair program. A small, personal goodbye gift in the form of a letter or small photo album with pictures from your time together is a great way to express your appreciation.

Message from John:

Coming back home was harder in some ways than going to Germany. It was difficult for me to leave the relationships that I had built there. In some ways, I have become a stranger in my own environment. A lot has changed since I left. But a lot has also stayed the same. I lost friends that couldn't cope with the changes and kept those who have grown with change.

Eventually that moment arrives. You board the plane and start the journey home. Don't expect to find everything the way it was when you left. Your family and friends will be excited to hear about your experiences and adventures. But this time will soon be over, and once again, normal everyday life will settle in. Be aware that your family and friends have also changed during your time abroad and have also experienced new things.

Message from John:

My year as an au pair is now a motivation for me to make sure I get my papers sorted out and finish what I started up there. Not many receive the chance that I got, and I'm determined to make the most of it.

FLY OUT there and stretch your wings: You will be surprised of how different the world is when you look at it from another angle... literally!

One Last Thing

If you've reached this point in the Au Pair Guide, you have collected a great deal of helpful tips and suggestions for your time abroad as an au pair. If you approach the other culture with openness and accept your host family's lifestyle without prejudice, there is very little that can keep you from having an amazing time abroad. You will gain many new and valuable life experiences during this time: some hard, some unusual and some very precious.

I hope you have an unforgettable time and that you return home with new confidence, a more diverse view of the world and refined language skills. And last but not least, I hope you enjoy every second of it!

Carmen Kurz

How to Properly Handle Children

As an au pair, you are being trusted with the most important people in the world: your host parent's children.

Your main priority is to watch out for them, protect them from danger and give them your full and undivided attention. Being an au pair is not hard work from a physical standpoint, but it can still be a very challenging job. Skim the pages in this section before departing on your journey and then read them closely and carefully shortly after your arrival in the host country. You most likely are already experienced in dealing with children and these tips will probably not be completely new to you. This chapter is meant to help if you ever find yourself stuck in a situation where you don't know how to react. It also aims to give you a better understanding of children and their unique needs. The children should see you as a friend – a big sister or brother. When your host parents aren't around, you of course become more than a friend and carry the responsibility for their wellbeing.

In many situations, your gut feeling will give you the best answer on how to behave and care for the children.

> *An au pair is never allowed to punish the host family's children with physical violence. This could lead to an immediate termination of your stay.*

Tips & Tricks

How Children Develop

The following text gives you an overview of a child's developmental phases – starting from a few weeks to seven years old. Of course, these general statements don't fit every child perfectly since every child develops at its own pace physically and emotionally. These are merely a helpful frame of reference.

0–6 Months

Infants have a strong need for loving physical contact and closeness as this gives them a feeling of safety and security. Every infant is unique even though they all look fairly similar at this young age. An infant has a lot of adjusting to do once it leaves the womb. The voice of the mother is about the only familiar thing to a newborn.

At about 3 to 6 months of age, babies start to smile, murmur and babble. They become more alert and show more interest in their environment. They are constantly discovering new stimuli with their five senses. As soon as they can grasp an object with their hand, you'll need to keep an eye on what they try to stick in their mouths. This flood of new experiences is also tiring, which is why infants spend a lot of time sleeping.

Bottle Feeding An infant's daily rhythm also includes numerous feeding times and diaper changes. This means you should know how to give a baby a bottle, change its diaper and put it to sleep. An age-appropriate diet is important for the development of an infant's immune system and intestinal flora. Be sure to check with your host parents what milk, baby food and fruit the infant is allowed to eat. When feeding the baby milk from a bottle, always ensure that the temperature of the milk isn't too hot or cold before giving it to the baby. The best way to check the milk's temperature is to drip a few drops onto the crook of your arm. Keep in mind that the baby should be burped one or two times during feeding. To do this, lean its breast up against your shoulder and carefully pat it on the back between its shoulder blades. Never give an infant a bottle while it is lying down. It could choke and have difficulty breathing.

Changing Diapers It really isn't easy to describe how to change a diaper – you simply have to practice it. The baby should be handled with care but also with enough firmness to maneuver it into the necessary positions. Never take your eyes off a baby on a changing table! There is a real danger that it could fall from the table while it is trying to turn or struggle about. It is safer to change an active, strong-willed infant on the

82

ground. A blanket and/or towel provide good cushion for the baby and protection for the flooring below should something not stay contained in the diaper.

When caring for infants, you shouldn't wear any watches, bracelets or dangling earrings. Sharp metal can easily injure a baby's delicate skin or, in the case of earrings, the baby could grab hold of them and potentially injure you.

Tips
&
Tricks

Tips for Entertaining an Infant

You can cuddle or snuggle with your host family's infant and you can pamper it with attention. The best way to entertain babies at this age is to hold or rock them lightly or to carry them around. As was mentioned above, they are primarily focused on their basic needs such as eating, drinking, sleeping and digesting. They are interested in sounds, tones, voices and colorful objects which they can grasp and they love playing with their own fingers and feet.

How to Calm a Baby Down If the baby doesn't stop crying you should first of all check if all of its basic needs have been met: Perhaps it is hungry, thirsty or is feeling too hot or cold. Maybe the baby has a wet diaper, an irritated butt or gas. Try some traditional methods for calming the baby such as a pacifier, physical contact or a light stomach massage. Turn on some music and walk or move rhythmically with the baby in your arms. Rocking the baby in its cradle can also be very helpful. If that doesn't work, put the baby in its bed for a couple of minutes and allow yourself a short break. Then try it again. If you get the feeling that all your endeavors are in vain, it is advisable to contact the parents.

6–12 Months

"Active" is the best word to describe babies at the age of 6-12 months. Their motor skills are developing quickly during this time. They crawl forwards and backwards, they learn how to sit on their own, pull themselves up on the furniture and have a knack for pulling things off of tables. They can climb up onto the couch while stairs are now viewed as fascinating obstacles that need to be overcome.

Putting on clothes and changing diapers is not as simple anymore, since the urge to discover and play has become the baby's top priority. Children learn how to say their first syllables at this age. They react to their name and also know the names of family members and pets. They may not yet be able to pronounce the names correctly, but you can often understand them with a little imagination. "Ma" stands for mommy und "Da" for daddy. Or perhaps they will come up with something else...

Teething also starts during this time. You can support this process by giving the baby hard cookies or a teething ring which will stimulate the jaw.

Children are now able to hold a bottle on their own are learning how to drink from a cup. If seated in a high chair during meals, it's often a good idea to buckle them in for safety reasons.

 Never turn your back on a baby in a highchair and never let them stand up in the highchair.

In order for both of you to stay clean while eating, tie a bib around the baby's neck and keep a towel within reach for yourself. Children can already hold a spoon by themselves at this age. But when they actually try to eat, half of the food will usually wind up someplace other than their mouth. That's why the little one needs your support; direct its hand firmly and with care.

Tips for Entertaining

Children songs and nursery rhymes are good entertainment for this age group. Children enjoy the sound of a familiar voice singing to them. You probably remember some songs from your own childhood such as "Twinkle, Twinkle Little Star" and "Itsy Bitsy Spider".

Children can participate more actively now when you play with them. Place a toy on the floor and let the child crawl towards it. Once it has reached its goal, it will certainly want to investigate the toy closely with its hands. Or hide a toy under a blanket and let the baby look for it. Simple ball games are also possible now: Roll a ball back and forth between you and the baby.

1–2 Years

Most children learn to walk when they are one year old. And before they turn three, they can already run pretty fast. Their curiosity knows no bounds and they love exploring their environment by putting everything into their mouth. At this point, you have to intervene more often and the child has to learn its first rules. After all, it doesn't know yet that the pretty red berries and the sweet-smelling detergent are poisonous. When you forbid them something, they will try to hit, kick or pinch you. But if you persevere you will receive a little "thank you" kiss and a hearty hug in the end.

Language The toddler's language skills are developing rapidly. At first, only those closest to them are able to understand their babbling. But gradually the little ones use more and more words and enjoy word games. They also discover the possibility of expressing their own will through language. When you tell them to do something, they will prefer doing the exact opposite or answer you with a "No". In order to direct their behavior successfully, you can easily distract them with a toy or lure them by suggesting a visit to the playground.

While exploring their environment, they have also discovered their independence –they now climb steep stairs without even thinking about how they will get back down again. They also enjoy looking out of the window and observing all the interesting things outside.

Never leave a child alone in a room with a window open. There is a danger that the child might climb up on furniture to look out of the window and lean too far out!

Tips & Tricks

Tips for Entertaining

At this age children can be both little monsters and cute bundles of joy. They love playing with the phone, with toy cars, dolls or shape games that can easily be taken apart and put together again. Another great activity is to build towers from building blocks and make them collapse again. When playing hide and seek with children this age, hide in a way so that parts of your body can still be seen. That way they can find you easily. It's always a good idea to read them a good night story from a nicely illustrated book when you bring them to bed. They will be fascinated by the colorful pictures while listening to your voice. You will probably have to read the same stories every night, because they are so beautiful and children love repetition. Your host family's child undoubtedly has a cuddly blanket or a favorite toy that it wants to take everywhere it goes – and especially to bed. It won't even think of sleeping without it.

Bathing a toddler takes some preparation and practice. Keep a big towel ready for the wet little body, ideally pre-warmed on the radiator. Fill the tub with water, but not too much. Check the water's temperature with your elbow – not with your hand. Try to play with the child while it is bathing. If a child is scared, it can be especially helpful to distract it with a little game.

Tips & Tricks

> *Warning: Never leave a child alone during bathing time – not even when the phone rings or when there is someone at the door!*

2–3 Years

Children at the age of 2 and 3 years can pronounce words relatively clearly and you will hear a clear "No" with increasing frequency. This is when they make their first attempts at dominating and giving orders – they can be pretty willful and stubborn. Are your rules being ignored? Is the child constantly pushing the limits? Welcome to the phase of defiance! Children this age are not yet able to express their precise needs with words. Instead they act defiantly in order to get your attention.

> *When children throw a tantrum, sometimes the best thing you can do is to ignore them for a while and just pretend that nothing happened.*

Tips & Tricks

Apart for "No", the second important word during this phase is "Why". The little ones are able to ask you questions until the cows come home. Try to support their language development by giving them detailed replies to their many questions.

Another important topic now is using the toilet. Ask your host family how they are teaching their child to use the toilet. Occasionally small accidents happen, of course, and you shouldn't make a big deal out of them. At the age of almost 3, children usually show a lot more self-control in this area.

Tips for Entertaining

Children this age enjoy playing with big piece puzzles and big building blocks. They can already hold thick colored pencils and wax crayons and they love drawing – not only on paper, but also on clothes, couches and walls. Their fine motor skills are increasing so that they are now able to thread big beads onto string or make objects with playdough. They are able to perceive more things now, which is why they enjoy looking at picture books even more than before. The little ones are fascinated by puppet shows, but their attention spans are still relatively short. They also get a kick out of making music on rhythmic instruments. The pots and pans from mom's kitchen should do for a start – assuming that mommy is okay with that. There are endless possibilities for keeping children entertained outside, for example with sand or water. A waterproof coverall is optimal in cold and wet weather.

3–4 Years

Most children go to a preschool at this age, where they learn to become part of a group. Many children make their first friends here and discover that it's actually fun to play with another child. As their fine motor skills improve, their scribble scrabble pictures become increasingly a thing of the past. Instead, they start to draw people, objects and landscapes. The little ones enjoy climbing and can keep their balance pretty well when jumping. Their perception has clearly improved, but they still need to be supervised carefully. When playing, it can easily happen that they run obliviously out onto the street or wander away from their parent's house without noticing.

Tips for Entertaining

Ball games are a popular activity for outdoors. Tricycles or little scooters are also a favorite means of transport for getting to the playground. The little ones enjoy playing with a toy supermarket or in their own "house". You can easily build such a house yourself by placing some chairs opposite each other and draping a blanket over them. Maybe there is a clothesline in the backyard where you can move your "house" outside in nice weather. Or make a bus by putting some chairs in a row. The child can be the bus driver and will take you, the teddy bear and a doll for a ride. They can also play simple, two person games, such as memory, now. In good weather, try to go for a walk with them as often as possible. The little hunters and collectors love to discover hidden treasures such as leaves, stones, sticks and pine cones. Children this age can be entertained for hours with crayons, paper, illustrated books, finger paint, chalk, blunt scissors and playdough.

Tips & Tricks

Be careful when it comes to scissors:
Aside from paper they can also cut hair and clothes.

4–5 Years

4–5-year-olds show considerably more independence. They no longer want to be treated like babies and want to do things their own way. They develop preferences and dislikes as it relates to food, playmates, clothing and toys and change their minds often in these areas without warning. At times they are cooperative and include you into their games while at other times they will exclude you. They have lots of imagination and love to role play, especially family roles (mother, father, child). They also enjoy dressing up like their parents.

Children this age will enjoy showing you where things are located around the house, help you prepare simple meals and tell you how things should be done. They can hop, jump and do somersaults. Of course, they are also able to kick, hit and throw various objects. Expressions of power and inappropriate behavior are new achievements that they love to bring out at exactly the wrong times. Talk to your host parents about how to handle these types of situations.

If a child is to be dropped off somewhere that usually means it also will need to be picked up. The person responsible for picking up the child should know the necessary information (time and place) for completing this task. Be careful though, as children can be very mischievous when they want to avoid going home and busy parents also occasionally forget to pass on information. This is why it is always a good idea to ask for the information you need and double-check things when in doubt.

Tips & Tricks

Tips for Entertaining

When reading to children in this age group, they will show an increasing interest in the letters and numbers that appear on the pages. You can play little word or number games with them and teach them how to write their own name. You can find a number of children's books at your local library – most even have a children's play area. Creative crafts are still popular at this age and they show significant improvement in their ability to translate their imaginative ideas into their creations. They also will show greater dedication and concentration on their work. Games that require no preparation or materials are ideal when travelling or taking walks. A game like "I spy with my little eye…" promotes communication and the recognition of colors and objects.

5–7 Years

Personality While the focus was on the development of motor and linguistic skills in the previous years, this period represents a shift towards personality development. The child now sees older family members as role models. You should be aware that your behavior is being closely observed and that your authority will be questioned at times. Be a responsible role model and take some time to explain your actions and decisions when the child makes critical comments. Children of this age are constantly making new contacts at school, which influences their social behaviors. When playing or working in a group, they learn to understand the gestures of others and develop a feel for justice and compassion. This age group tends to be very independent and can generally take care of their own needs pretty well at this point. Eating with a knife and fork, bathing on their own and brushing their teeth should be no problem at this stage.

When it comes to checking whether teeth have been brushed, trust is nice, but monitoring is better!

Tips & Tricks

The need to take on responsibility and participate in the world of grown-ups will continually grow now. You can give children in this age group little tasks to complete, such as feeding the rabbits, getting the mail or watering the flowers. Praise for a job well done lets them know you care. This process bolsters the child's self-confidence and encourages it to do these tasks with great concentration and dedication.

Tips for Entertaining
You will need far less time when it comes to entertaining kids of this age. They often find ways to busy themselves on their own or with friends. Your job is more to observe and make sure they don't get into trouble. You have to know when the child is at a friend's house and when it is supposed to be back. It is important that you let the child know where its boundaries are and that you stick to these boundaries. If the child doesn't uphold these rules, tell it what it did wrong.
At the age of 6, kids begin to understand the concept of time. Explain what a second, minute and hour is.
It could be that your host family's child loves playing with you, or with

its friends or by itself. Girls can occupy themselves for hours with their Barbie dolls – changing their outfits and brushing their hair. Boys prefer to energetically play in the role of their favorite action heroes. When the weather is bad, board games are a good way to pass the time indoors.

"One of the biggest highlights for me was when my host family's child came to me, took me in his arms and told me that he really liked me."

Stephan, au pair in UK

What Preferences Do Your Host Family's Children Have?

We've provided you with space here to record the various characteristics and preferences of the children in your host family. What stage of development are they in at the moment? What do they like to do? What are their hobbies? What do they like to eat? What are the names of their friends? Do they have any allergies or chronic illnesses? What strengths and weaknesses do they have? Knowing the preferences of the children you're caring for is a big help and will make your job a lot easier.

Children	Preferences

Rhymes and Fingerplay

Below are a few popular nursery rhymes and fingerplay. Even if your host children won't understand the text, you can be sure that they will enjoy them. When playing with small children, enthusiasm and loving attention are the keys. Rhythm and hand motions are also helpful when it comes to songs and fingerplay.

Rhymes and Fingerplays	Guidance
One, two, three, four, five	Count fingers on one hand
Once I caught a fish alive	Close hands pretending to catch a fish
Six, seven, eight, nine, ten	Count fingers on one hand
Then I let it go again	Open closed hands and spread arms a little
Why did you let it go?	Spread arms as if questioning someone
Because it bit my finger so	Shake hand as if it is hurt
Which finger did it bite?	Spread arms as if questioning someone
This little finger on the right	Wiggle little finger
The eensy, weensy spider	Make climbing motion, alternating index finger
Climbed up the water spout	and thumb of opposite hands
Down came the rain	Make raindrops falling down
And washed the spider out	Push hands to side
Out came the sun	Hands make a circle over head
And dried up all the rain	With palms in front, wave side to side in drying
And the eensy, weensy spider	motion
Climbed up the spout again	Repeat climbing motion
Five red apples	Five fingers held up
Hanging on a tree	
The juiciest apples	
You ever did see!	
The wind came past	
And gave an angry frown	Shake head and look angry
And one little apple	
Came tumbling down!	
Four red apples, etc.	

Counting-out Rhyme

Five little monkeys
jumping on the bed
One fell off
and bumped his head
Mama called the doctor
and the doctor said:
No more monkeys
jumping on the bed!

Four little monkeys
jumping on the bed
One fell off...

Eeny, meeny, miny, moe,
Catch a tiger by the toe.
If he hollers, let him go,
Eeny, meeny, miny, moe.

One little flower, one little bee.
One little blue bird, high in the tree.
One little brown bear smiling at me.
One is the number I like,
you see.

Rich Man, Poor Man,
Beggar Man, Thief,
Doctor, Lawyer,
Indian Chief.

One little, two little, three little Indians
Four little, five little, six little Indians
Seven little, eight little, nine little Indians
Ten little Indian boys.
Ten little, nine little, eight little Indians
Seven little, six little, five little Indians
Four little, three little, two little Indians
One little Indian boy.

Five little ducks
Went out one day
Over the hill and far away
Mother Duck said:
Quack, quack, quack, quack
But only four little ducks
Came waddling back

Four little ducks
Went out one day
Over the hill and far away
Mother Duck said:
Quack, quack, quack, quack
But only three little ducks
Came waddling back.
(And so on)

Sad Mother Duck
Went out one day
Over the hill and far away
Sad Mother Duck said:
Quack, quack, quack.
And all of the five
Little ducks came back.

A Short Introduction on Caring for Sick Children

Children are particularly susceptible to sicknesses during their early years since their immune system hasn't fully developed yet. However, an only child that spends most of its time at home will generally be sick less often than a child that goes to preschool every day and is in regular contact with other children.

Since there is a good chance that your host family's children will eventually get sick during your stay, you should at least have a basic knowledge of the main illnesses that a child can come down with. Most of them are not serious and can be easily treated.

In general, a healthy immune system needs:

- A healthy and nutritious diet

- Affectionate care

- Restful sleep

- Movement and fresh air

A child is unable to describe its needs, pains and feelings as articulately as an adult can. As a result, caring for a child requires some perception and attentive observation.

Sick children can be unpredictable and need a risk-free environment. Keep medications stored in a childproof place and use good common sense to ensure that the child both feels safe and is safe!

Here is a list of the most common childhood illnesses, their symptoms and corresponding treatments. These are only general guidelines and helpful tips for caring for sick children. Always follow the treatment guidelines laid out by your host parents and the child's doctor!

Fever

On its own, a fever is not an illness. It is only a symptom that signals that the immune system is reacting to something. It could be fighting a virus or bacterial infection.

Small rises in temperature can also come from physical activity, being too warmly dressed or exposure to a hot environment. If you think one of these factors may be behind the child's warmer temperatures, make the necessary adjustments (take a break, drink some water, unzip the jacket, go inside, etc.) and check the child's temperature again after a few minutes. A healthy child's temperature should be somewhere between 97.5 and 99.5 °F (36.5 – 37.5 °C).

The Fahrenheit scale is mainly used in the US while just about every other country uses the Celsius scale. If you are unsure which scale is being used, ask to be sure.

32 °F is equal to 0 °C. The conversion formula is as follows:

$$°F = °C \times 1.8 + 32$$

$$°C = (°F - 32) : 1.8$$

Celsius	Fahrenheit
over 40 °C	over 104 °F
38.5 – 40 °C	101.3 – 104 °F
37.9 – 38.4 °C	100.2 – 101.1 °F
37.5 – 37.8 °C	99.5 – 100.1 °F
< 37.5 °C	< 99.5 °F

Taking a Child's Temperature

A person's body temperature changes throughout the day. The temperature is lowest between 6 am and 7 am and highest at around 4 pm or 5 pm. Modern temperature taking methods that use the forehead or inner ear to take a person's temperature are popular, but their accuracy is disputed.

Rectal

The most exact temperatures are taken rectally (anally). To perform this type of measurement, place the infant or toddler on its back. Its legs should be bent with the thighs lightly pressed up against the stomach. Smear some Vaseline on the tip of the thermometer. This will help minimize discomfort. For older children, this method can also be done while they lay on their side.

Sublingual

Taking a temperature by placing a thermometer under the tongue is recommended for older children. The temperatures will generally be about 0.5 °F (0.3 °C) lower than when using the rectal method.

Axillar

One can also take a child's temperature by placing a thermometer under their armpit. This is another good method for older children. Make sure that the armpit is dry and that the tip of the thermometer is at the center of the armpit. The temperatures will generally be about 0.9 °F (0.5 °C) lower than when using the rectal method.

At What Point Should I Call a Doctor?

Usually the host parents will decide when to call a doctor. But if you are alone with a child who has fallen ill and are unsure of what to do, these are good general guidelines for helping you make the right decision.

Call a doctor immediately, if:

- A child less than 3 months old has a temperature above 101.3 °F (38.5 °C)

- A child of any age has a fever of 104 °F (40 °C) or higher

- The child has a fever and is difficult to awaken

- The child has feverish (febrile) spasms

- The child's neck is stiff or the fontanelle (the soft spot between the skull bones on infants) is bulging

Call a doctor within 24 hours, if

- The fever is at or above 101.3 °F (38.5° C), especially if the child is younger than 2 years old

- The child experiences a painful or burning sensation when urinating or if its urine smells acrid

- The child has had a fever for longer than 24 hours without any obvious cause

Measures for Combating a Fever

No major measures must be taken for body temperatures up to 101.3 °F (38.5° C). In such cases, the child needs rest and should be drinking plenty of liquids.

For temperatures beyond this, a doctor should be consulted. Physical measures like applying damp cloths or cold compresses can help lower the body's temperature. However, cold compresses should never be used when the fever is still rising. This would simply cause the fever to rise further as the body reacts to the cold temperatures.

Stage of Fever	Symptoms	Measures
Rising fever	Chills Shivers	Supply heat Warm beverages Hot-water bottle Warm blankets
Fever peak	Accelerated breathing Restlessness	Loving care Applying damp cloths Cold compresses Thin blankets, so that heat isn't trapped A dark, quiet environment
Receding fever	Sweating	Provide plenty of liquids Thin clothing Change clothing when necessary
Exhaustion	Extreme fatigue	Peace and quiet Rest Observation

Infants and toddlers can come down with a fever if they haven't had enough to drink. This is what is called thirst fever. This is why it is always important to monitor whether an infant or toddler is getting enough to drink. A longer lasting fever can lead to dehydration.

The Common Cold

You are surely familiar with the symptoms of a cold. Along with a stuffy nose, coughing and a sore throat, a cold can also lead to exhaustion, chills or even a fever.

Treatment

- Keep the child from any strenuous activities.

- Offer the child plenty to drink as this facilitates the discharge of phlegm through coughing.

- To keep the mucous membranes from drying out, try to keep the child in a humid environment. Use humidifiers or place wet towels on the heaters.

- For sniffles

    1. Apply mild nose drops or a saline solution (½ tea spoon of salt mixed into 0.5 l of water).

    2. Infrared light therapy – please follow the instructions provided with the lamp.

    3. For older children, a vapor bath can be helpful. Fill a large bowl with hot water. Have the child hold their head above the bowl and breathe the steam in. If the child doesn't mind, place a towel over its head so that the steam stays more concentrated. This can be done multiple times a day. A session usually lasts about 5 – 10 minutes. **Be careful:** The water is very hot and could scald you or the child!

Part III A Short Introduction on Caring for Sick Children

- For sore throats

    1. Offer the child cough drops to suck on. **Be careful:** Children under the age of 4 can choke on cough drops!

    2. A warm neck wrap is a pleasant and soothing option (see hot and cold therapy on page 116. The wrap can be worn during sleep or during a break from activity. The child can wear it for as long as it likes. When removing the wrap, make sure that the neck is dry.

To minimize the risk of scalding, use a thermos when making a vapor bath. Fill it up about half way and place it under the child's nose.

Tips & Tricks

Bronchitis

Bronchitis is an inflammation of the upper respiratory tract with symptoms similar to a cold. Initial dry coughs change over time to coughs where mucus is expectorated (coughed up). Loss of appetite, lack of energy, pain in the breast area and a rattling sound when breathing are also common symptoms of bronchitis.

Treatment

- Keep the child from any strenuous activities.

- If the child is running a fever, it should stay in bed.

- Offer the child plenty to drink as this facilitates the discharge of phlegm through coughing.

- Give the child a vapor bath (see treatment for the common cold).

102

- To keep the mucous membranes from drying out, try to keep the child in a humid environment. Use humidifiers or place wet towels on the heaters.

- Breathing exercises help relieve certain symptoms and can help the child breathe more easily. You can make a game out of these exercises by having the child blow up balloons, blow soap bubbles or blow a cotton ball back and forth across a table.

The child needs to see a doctor if the bronchitis symptoms haven't cleared up after 2-3 days, if it has a fever above 101.3 °F (38.5 °C), if it has difficulty breathing or if it is coughing up pus or blood.

Middle Ear Infection

A middle ear infection is often a secondary condition resulting from infections in the nose/throat area. It is caused by bacterial or viral pathogens. Its symptoms include restlessness, loss of appetite, ear pain, fever and difficulty hearing as well as whimpering and crying in infants due to the pain.

Treatment

- Apply mild nose drops or a saline solution (½ tea spoon of salt mixed in 0.5 l of water) to help keep the middle ear ventilated.

- Other treatments include the use of an onion bag or infrared light therapy (see hot and cold therapy on page 116.

A doctor should be consulted immediately if a child is thought to have a middle ear infection.

Gastroenteritis/Diarrhea and Vomiting

Gastroenteritis can be caused by bacterial or viral pathogens. Typical symptoms include vomiting, diarrhea with mostly fluid stool, stomach aches, cramps and moderate fever.

Treatment

- If the child is running a fever, it should stay in bed.

- Offer the child plenty to drink – herbal teas or fruit teas are a good choice.

- If the child is hungry, offer light foods, such as zwieback, porridge, grated apple (with skin), smashed banana, crisp bread, pretzel sticks or mashed potatoes.

- In the case of severe vomiting, do not give the child anything to eat. Instead, it should try to drink fluids (tea or water) until things settle down.

- Wash your hands thoroughly and regularly so that you don't infect yourself or others.

Due to the loss of water and minerals, a person – particularly infants and toddlers – can quickly become dehydrated. If this occurs, a doctor should be consulted.

Eye Infection/Conjunctivitis

Conjunctivitis can be broken down into two types: contagious and non-contagious. Non-contagious conjunctivitis is usually caused by an allergic reaction or irritants such as heat, dust or dry air, while contagious conjunctivitis is caused by germs. Symptoms include itchy, watery eyes, burning sensations in the eye and swelling. Eyes can also become red, sensitive to light or secrete greenish discharges.

Treatment

- Gently rinse the eye with water or a saline solution (½ tea spoon of salt mixed in 0.5 l of water). Please do not use a chamomile solution as chamomile can irritate the eye!

- For non-contagious conjunctivitis, pharmacies and drugstores carry non-prescription eye drops (please follow the product's instructions carefully).

A contagious case of conjunctivitis should be treated by a doctor.

Measles

Measles is very contagious and the virus is quickly spread by airborne transmission (coughing, sneezing, etc.)

The early stages of measles are very similar to a cold with symptoms like sniffles, low fever, sore throat, general feelings of illness and coughing. On the second or third day, small white spots appear on the oral membrane near the molars and the fever begins to recede. Soon, the fever returns and the typical measles rash begins to spread throughout the body, starting at the head. The rash starts out as large, dark red spots that later fade. The skin then turns dry and flaky during the recovery phase.

Treatment

- Plenty of rest and quiet is recommended.

- Since it is very contagious, the child must be kept isolated.

- Further treatment depends on the symptoms occurring.

The child should see a doctor if measles is suspected.

Mumps

The mumps virus is easily spread by airborne transmission (sneezing, coughing, etc.).

Sometimes a mumps infection does not result in any negative symptoms. Typical symptoms include loss of appetite, sore throat, headaches, fatigue, fever and a swelling of the parotid glands (chubby cheeks).

Treatment

- Since this is a contagious virus, the child should get plenty of rest in isolation.

- Make sure that the child regularly brushes its teeth. This disinfects the mouth and helps prevent salivary gland infections.

- As chewing and swallowing can be painful with mumps, it is best to offer fluid or soft foods (mashed potatoes, soups, porridge).

The child should see a doctor if mumps is suspected.

Rubella/German Measles

The rubella virus can be recognized by a light fever, a swelling of the lymph nodes and a red rash, which spreads across the entire body within a few hours. This illness often comes and goes without any major negative symptoms, which is why children often don't complain of feeling sick.

Treatment

- The child should be isolated from other children.

- It should get adequate rest and not engage in too much physical activity.

- Further treatment depends on the symptoms occurring.

The child should see a doctor if rubella is suspected.

Head Lice

Head lice are parasites that usually spread by direct head to head contact, though they can be passed on through clothing or bedding. Head lice infections generally occur with children.

The main symptom is an itchy head, which is caused by the parasite's bite. A rash-like appearance can become visible on the back of the head or neck after a while as well as small wounds on the scalp from frequent scratching. The lice are generally only visible with a magnifying glass, but their white eggs (nits) are easier to spot, especially on darker hair.

Treatment

- Effective insecticides are available at most drugstores in gel, powder or emulsion form. Please follow the instructions carefully! The treatment should be repeated after 8-10 days. Brushes and combs should also be treated with the insecticide.

- Caps, jackets with hoods and pillowcases should be washed separately at a temperature of at least 140 °F (60 °C). Non-washable materials can be placed in a freezer for 24 hours or sealed in airtight vacuum bags for a week, which should kill off any lice.

- The child should generally stay home. In many countries, head lice cases are viewed as an infectious disease and children are not allowed to attend school while infected.

- If one person in the family becomes infected, every member of the family should be checked for head lice. It is also recommended to engage in preventative treatment.

Never give a child medication unless you have received previous instructions from the parents or a doctor. Medication should be administered carefully in accordance with the instructions (dosage, schedule). Some medications aren't very tasty. Perhaps the parents or doctor can provide some tips on how to best administer the medication.

Make sure that medications are completely closed and securely stored out of the reach of children.

First Aid for Children

While sicknesses represent one type of potential danger to a child's health, there are other types as well: accidents around the house for example. Children are especially at-risk as they have not yet learned how to watch out for their own safety. Curiosity mixed with a lack of experience means that children will regularly put themselves in dangerous situations without even realizing it. This is why children should be taught to recognize and avoid dangerous situations at the earliest possible age.

The following is a short overview of the most common accidents that occur with children as well as notes on which first aid measures should be taken. Further tips can be found on the internet, for example on the Red Cross website at www.redcross.org. They also offer first aid apps that you can download for your smartphone.

Nosebleeds

Nosebleeds are a fairly common occurrence with children. They can result from horseplay, falling on one's face or cleaning one's nose too forcefully.

Measures

- Have the child tilt their head forward, which helps to control the flow of blood.

- Put a cold compress around the child's neck to constrict the blood vessels.

- For more serious nosebleeds, you should pinch and hold the nose shut with your fingers.

Wounds

Abrasions and scrapes are a part of a child's everyday life.

Measures

- Small surface wounds generally heal on their own. To help console the child, it often helps to cover the wound with a colorful bandage.

- Dirty wounds should be cleaned under running water (clean, drinking water) and possibly treated with disinfectant.

- Large, heavily bleeding wounds should be treated by a doctor. As an initial first aid measure, the wound should be covered with a sterile compress. A compression bandage with gauze can be used to stop the bleeding. If the wound requires stitching, this should be administered within 6 hours. After 6 hours, stitching is often no longer possible and a noticeable scar remains.

If the wound bleeds heavily with a sizable gash of notable depth or breadth, a doctor is required for closing the wound. Stitching it together will reduce the possibility of an infection and speed up recovery. Only a small scar is left behind. Smaller wounds are generally glued or stapled together by emergency room surgeons/physicians.

110

Blocked Windpipe

This emergency situation can occur very easily with infants and toddlers. Infants can choke on their own vomit, while toddlers can choke on candies or small toys.

The symptoms include wide open eyes, a nearly silent struggle for breath, forceful coughing, pain when swallowing or lips that begin to turn blue.

Measures

- Hold the infant or toddler by their feet so that their upper body hangs towards the ground. Often, this will help them spit out the object on their own.

- For older children, bend them over your knee and slap them on the back between the shoulder blades.

- If these do not work, call the emergency medical services!

It is helpful to place a rolled up towel behind the back of a sleeping infant so that they lay somewhat on their side. This helps keep the windpipe open should the infant vomit during sleep.

Insect Bite or Sting

An insect bite or sting is always an uncomfortable situation. The skin swells, turns red and the spot of the bite begins to itch. If the child has an allergic reaction to this type of bite or sting, it can lead to nausea, vomiting and dizziness.

Measures

- Remove the stinger from the wound.

- If the child is unable to do so, suck on the wound to remove any residual venom.

- Put drops of onion juice or vinegar on the wound.

- Cooling the wound with cold, wet cloths, ice cubes or cold packs also helps relieve discomfort.

- A doctor should be called immediately for insect bites or stings inside the mouth! To keep the windpipe open, the child should continuously suck on ice cubes. You should also wrap a cold, wet towel around the child's neck.

Burns/Scalds

The stove, oven, BBQ or clothes iron are the typical sites around the house where burn injuries take place. The intensity of a burn is classified into three categories:

1st degree burn: The skin swells and turns red; the person feels pain

2nd degree burn: The skin swells and turns red; blisters form and the person feels pain

3rd degree burn: Skin tissue is destroyed with visible charring and scabbing

Measures

- For a first degree burn, place the affected area under cold, running water until the pain subsides or apply cold, wet compresses.

- For second and third degree burns, cover any open wounds with a sterile compress and seek medical help.

- Should a child's clothing catch fire, you can put the fire out by either dousing the person with water or wrapping them up in a woolen blanket.

Bone Fractures

A broken bone is generally recognizable from the abnormal position of a body part and its limited mobility or complete immobility. This is generally accompanied by swelling and intense pain. If the child is not in pain but is still unable to move the affected body part or moves it in a protective or unnatural way, you should continue to treat the injury as a possible fracture.

Measures

- The body part should be immobilized.

- For fractures with a wound, cover the wound with a sterile cloth or compress.

- If you cannot bring the child to the doctor or hospital yourself, you should call for an ambulance.

Emergency Numbers for Traditional Au Pair Countries

Country	Police	Ambulance	Fire Service
Australia	000	000	000
Germany	110	112	112
France	17	15	18
Great Britain	999	999	999
Ireland	999	999	999
Italy	113	118	115
New Zealand	111	111	111
Spain	112	112	112
USA	911	911	911

Hot and Cold Therapy

The therapeutic effect of heat and cold has been recognized for over a thousand years. These methods are simple to apply, require little preparation and are generally very cheap. Test these methods out on your own body so that you know how they feel and how to regulate intensity and other factors. These nursing measures provide the host family's sick child with loving attention, which also has a healing effect.

Heat Applications

Heat therapy helps promote circulation, stimulate the metabolism and relieve chronic pain.

Hot-water Bottle

Fill a hot-water bottle made of rubber half-way up with warm or hot water. Before closing the bottle, squeeze the remaining air out of it. This allows the bottle to remain flexible and optimally adapt to various positions. Hot-water bottles for children usually have a soft cloth cover that protects their skin from irritations and burns. Never use boiling water to fill the bottle!

Cherry Pit Bags/Rice Sacks

Cherry pit bags or rice sacks can be bought or made at home. To make one yourself, you need either clean cherry pits or rice and a cloth bag (socks also work well) to seal them in. To heat them up, you can either put them in the oven (at a temperature no higher than 140 °F / 60 °C) or put them in the microwave. Combined with a message, this can be a very effective and relaxing treatment.

Warm Wraps

A warm wrap consists of two towels or rags, which are ideally made from natural materials (cotton or linen). You can use hankies, small towels or wash rags.

Wet one rag with warm to hot water and wring it out so that it is warm to the touch but not dripping wet. Lay it in the second rag/towel and wrap it around the affected body part. You can also use herbal tea (chamomile or thyme) on the first rag to give it a pleasant smell.

Be careful about using essential oils for this purpose though, as they can irritate the skin as well as the mucous membranes of the eyes and nose.

Onion Bag

Heat therapy with an onion bag is used to combat middle ear infections.

Cut a raw onion into thin strips and heat it in the oven for 10-15 minutes at 300 °F (150 °C). Once this is done, put the onion pulp into a rag and bind it so that the onion cannot escape. If the child is receptive to the idea, you can place the "bag" on the infected ear. If the child doesn't want it directly on the ear, you can try placing it next to the ear.

The therapy is especially suitable for night while the child is sleeping. The only negative is that children often don't like the oniony smell.

Infrared Light

When using an infrared light for treatment, you need to follow the instructions provided with the device. Note the correct distance between the lamp and the affected body part, the recommended treatment times as well as the intensity settings for the lamp. If used incorrectly, an infrared light can easily burn a child's sensitive skin.

When using heat therapy, you should always regularly check to see if any notable changes are taking place at the affected area, such as redness or blisters. Warm wraps and cherry pit/rice bags are also an ideal therapy for calming jittery and restless children.

Cold Applications

Cold therapy is used to absorb heat and relieve acute pain stemming from bruises or sprains while also providing an anti-inflammatory effect. It can also help slow blood flow in the case of major wounds.

Cold Compresses

Take a dish towel and moisten it with warm or cool water (not freezing cold water!). Toddlers and infants are very sensitive to temperature, so you can simply use room temperature water when treating children of a young age. Place the wet towel along the calf and wrap another dry towel around it to hold it in place. Remove the towels when the cooling effect dissipates or if the child finds the compress uncomfortable.

Cold Washcloths

Moisten a wash rag with cold water and wring it out. Use the rag to dab or press against the affected area. This method is very simple and effective for smaller injuries.

Gel Packs

Many households have a gel pack or other cooling element ready for use in their refrigerator or freezer. For short periods,

the gel pack can be applied directly to the affected area. If you will be using the pack for more than a few minutes, you should wrap it in a towel. Otherwise the extreme cold could have a negative effect on blood flow to the area.

Ice Bags

Fill a zipper bag (3l size) half way up with crushed ice and seal it. Wrap a towel around the bag to prevent an overcooling of the skin.

If you don't have access to any crushed ice, you can use a few ice cubes and add some water to the bag. The ice cubes will slowly melt while the water allows the bag to conform to the contours of the affected area.

If you are in a situation where you need something cold, but don't have any of the usual cooling elements handy, take a sealed food package from the refrigerator or freezer. Preferably something that fits the contours of the affected area.

Thanks

I would like to thank everyone who helped make this book possible.

Special thanks to:

- My partner and my son – for the patience and understanding they have shown me over the years

- Colleagues around the world – for their feedback on au pair programs in their respective countries

- All the au pairs and host families – for their willingness to participate in this book by writing short texts or providing quotes and for sharing their experiences with me

Thank you!

Au Pair Dictionary

Shortcuts: m = Masculinum; f = Femininum; n = Neutrum; pl = Plural

English	Spanish	French	German
accomodation	alojamiento (m)	logement (m)	Unterkunft (f)
account	cuenta (f)	compte (m) en banque	Konto (n)
afternoon nap	siesta (f)	sieste (f)	Mittagsschlaf (m)
agreement, arrangement	acuerdo (m)	l'accord (m)	Absprache (f)
aid	ayuda (f)	aide (f)	Mithilfe (f)
appreciation	estimación (f)	appréciation (f)	Wertschätzung (f)
arrival	llegada (f)	l'arrivée (f)	Anreise (f)
attention	atención (f)	attention (f)	Aufmerksamkeit (f)
autonomy, independence	independencia (f)	être indépendant (adj)	Selbstständigkeit (f)
available places	plazas disponibles	places (f, pl) disponibles	freie Plätze (f, pl)
baby	bebé (m)	nourrisson (m)	Säugling (m)
baby food	alimento (m) para bebés	pot (m) de bébé	Babynahrung (f)
bedding	sabana (f)	draps (m, pl)	Bettzeug (n)
bedrest	reposo (m) en cama	repos (m)	Bettruhe (f)
bib	babero (m)	bavoir (m)	Lätzchen (n)
bite	picadura (f) de insecto (m)	piqûre (f) d'insecte (f)	Insektenstich (m)
blabbing	chachára (f)	papotage (m)	Plapperei (f)
blood heat, body temperature	temperatura corporal (f)	température (f)	Körpertemperatur (f)

English	Spanish	French	German
blunt scissors	tijeras (f) deafiladas	ciseaux (m, pl) ronds	stumpfe Schere (f)
breathlessness	disnea(f)	difficultés respiratoire (f)	Atemnot (f)
buggy, pram	cochecito (m)	poussette (f)	Kinderwagen (m)
careful	con cuidado	avec soin	sorgfältig
catering	comida (f)	nourriture (f)	Verpflegung (f)
cereal	muesli (m) / cereales	céréales (f, pl)	Müsli (n)
chalk	tiza (f)	craie (f)	Kreide (f)
class, tuition	clase (f)	cours (m, pl)	Unterricht (m)
cold	resfriado (m)	rhume (m)	Schnupfen (m)
congestion	estreñimiento (m)	constipation (f)	Verstopfung (f)
consultation	consulta (f)	consultation (f)	Rücksprache (f)
crayons	lapices (m) de color	crayons (m, pl) de couleur	Buntstifte (f, pl)
cuddly blanket	manta (f)	doudou (m)	Schmusedecke (f)
culture shock	choque cultural (m)	choc (m) culturel	Kulturschock (m)
cup	taza (f)	tasse (f)	Tasse (f)
curious	curioso (m), curiosa (f)	curieux	neugierig
cuss	palabrota (f)	gros mot (m)	Schimpfwort (n)
daily routine	rutina diaria (f)	déroulement (m) de la journée	Tagesablauf (m)
defiant phase	período (m) de terquedad (f)	bouder (verb)	Trotzphase (f)
departure	salida (f)	départ (m)	Abreise (f)

English	Spanish	French	German
diaper, nappy	pañales (m)	couches (m, pl)	Windeln (f, pl)
diarrhea	diarrea (f)	diarrhée (f)	Durchfall (m)
diatribe	crítica (w) fuerte o aguda	critique (f) sévère	heftige Kritik (f)
disappointment	desilusión (f)	déception (f)	Enttäuschung (f)
disease	enfermedad (f)	maladie (f)	Krankheit (f)
dish washer	lavavajillas (m)	lave (m) vaisselle	Geschirrspülmaschine (f)
distraction	distracción (f)	distraction (f)	Ablenkung (f)
dryer	secador (m)	sèche-linge (m)	Trockner (m)
duties	el deber (m)	devoir (m)	Pflichten (f, pl)
exhausting	agotador (m), agotadora	fatigant	anstrengend
failure	el fracaso (m)	échec (m)	Misserfolg (m)
fair comment	crítica constructiva (f)	critique (f) positive	sachliche Kritik (f)
fee	tasa (f)	frais (m, pl)	Gebühr (f)
fever	fiebre (f)	fièvre (f)	Fieber (n)
flatulence, winds	tener gases	ballonnement (m, pl)	Blähungen (f)
fork	tenedor (m)	fourchette (f)	Gabel (f)
free	gratis	gratuit	kostenlos
fridge	nevera (f)	frigo (m)	Kühlschrank (m)
frustration	frustración (f)	frustration (f)	Frustration (f)
glass	vaso (m)	verre (m)	Glas (n)
handling	el trato (m)	manière (f) de faire	Umgang (m)
headlice	piojo (m)	poux (m, pl)	Kopfläuse (f, pl)
high chair	sillita (f) de comer	chaise (f) haute	Kinderhochstuhl (m)

English	Spanish	French	German
homesickness	nostalgia	mal (m) du pays	Heimweh (n)
host family	familia anfitriona (f)	famille (f) d'accueil	Gastfamilie (f)
household	hogar (m)	foyer (m)	Haushalt (m)
housekeeping money	dinero para los gastos domésticos (m)	budget (m)	Haushaltsgeld (n)
immunisation, vaccination	vacunación (f)	vaccin (m)	Impfung (f)
infant, toddler	párvulo (m)	enfant (m) en bas âge	Kleinkind (n)
inflammation	inflamación (f)	inflammation (f)	Entzündung (f)
irresponsible	irresponsable	irresponsable	unverantwortlich
itch	picor (m)	démangeaison (f)	Juckreiz (m)
knife	cuchillo (m)	couteau (m)	Messer (n)
language course	un curso de idiomas (m)	cours (m) de langue	Sprachkurs (m)
language skills	los conocimientos del idioma	connaissances (f, pl) linguistiques	Sprachkenntnisse (f, pl)
laundry	ropa (f)	linge (m)	Wäsche (f)
mattress	el colchón (m)	matelas (m)	Matratze (f)
maturity	madurez (f)	maturité (f)	Reife (f)
measles	sarampión (m)	rougeole (f)	Masern (f)
misunderstanding	el malentendido (m)	malentendu (m)	Missverständnis (n)
molester	perturbador (m)	perturbateur (m)	Störenfried (m)
moody	mañoso/a	lunatique, sauts d'humeur	launisch

English	Spanish	French	German
mumps	parótiditis (f)	oreillons (m, pl)	Mumps (m)
musical clock	reloj de música	boîte (f) à musique	Spieluhr (f)
need, requirement	necesidad (f)	nécessité (f)	Bedürfnis (n)
nosebleed	hemorragia nasal (f)	saigner du nez (m)	Nasenbluten (n)
nursery rhyme	rima (f) infantil	comptine (f)	Kinderreim (m)
nutrition	alimentación (f)	alimentation(f)	Ernährung (f)
odd	raro (m), rara (f)	étrange	merkwürdig
openness	franqueza (f)	être ouvert (adj)	Aufgeschlossenheit (f)
overchallenged	no dar abasto	surchargé	überfordert
pacifier, dummy	chupete (m)	tétine (f)	Schnuller (m)
pain	dolor (m)	douleur (f)	Schmerz (m)
parenting	educación (f)	éducation (f)	Kindererziehung (f)
patch	curita (f)	pansement (m)	Pflaster (n)
patience	paciencia (f)	patience (f)	Geduld (f)
plasticine	plastilina (f)	pâte (f) à modeler	Knete (f)
plate	plato (m)	assiette (f)	Teller (m)
punctuality	puntualidad (f)	ponctualité (f)	Pünktlichkeit (f)
receipt, cash voucher	ticket (m)	ticket (m) de caisse	Kassenbeleg (m)
refusal	rechazo (m)	refus (m)	Ablehnung (f)
reserve assets	ahorros (m)	réserves (f, pl)	Rücklagen (f)
responsibility	responsabilidad (f)	responsabilité (f)	Verantwortung (f)
restroom	aseo (m)	toilettes (f, pl)	Toilette (f)

English	Spanish	French	German
riddle	enigma (m)	énigme (f)	Rätsel (n)
rights	derechos	droits (m, pl)	Rechte (f, pl)
rubella	rubéola (f)	rubéole (f)	Röteln (f, pl)
rules	reglas (f, pl)	règles (f, pl)	Regeln (f, pl)
scar	cicatriz (f)	cicatrice (f)	Narbe (f)
school certificate	hoja (w) de estudios	certificat (m) de fin d'étude	Schulzeugnis (n)
seatbelt	cinturón (m) de seguridad	ceinture (f) de sécurité	Sicherheitsgurt (m)
segregation, separation	separación (f)	séparation (f)	Trennung (f)
site map	mapa (m)	plan (m) de ville	Ortsplan (m)
snack	merienda (f)	goûter (m)	kleine Mahlzeit (f)
sore throat	dolor (m) de garganta (f)	mal (m) de gorge	Halsschmerzen (f, pl)
spasm	calambre (m)	crampe (f)	Krampf (m)
spoon	cuchara (f)	cuillère (f)	Löffel (m)
stubborn	terco/a	obtus	stur, hartnäckig
tantrum	arranque (m) de cólera (f)	coup (m) de colère (f)	Wutanfall (m)
tender	cariñosa (f)	tendrement	liebevoll
time difference	diferencia (w) de hora	décalage (m) horaire	Zeitverschiebung (f)
timetable	el horario (m)	emploi (m) du temps	Stundenplan (m)
to absorb	tragarse	avaler	verschlucken
to argue	disputar	se disputer	streiten
to be feverish	tener fiebre	avoir de la fièvre	Fieber haben

English	Spanish	French	German
to choke	asfixiarse	s'étouffer	ersticken
to calm a child	calmar a alguien	calmer, apaiser	Kind beruhigen
to clear the table	quitar la mesa	débarrasser la table	Tisch abräumen
to comfort	consolar a alguien	consoler	trösten
to cough	toser	tousser	husten
to dig	cavar	creuser	buddeln
to dusk	quitar el polvo	enlever la poussière	Staub wischen
to fool	engañar a alguien	tromper, tricher	austricksen
to govern	imponer reglas	imposer des règles	regeln
to hoover	pasar la aspiradora	passer l'aspirateur	Staub saugen
to lecture	leer algo en voz alta	lire une histoire	vorlesen
to mop	pasar la fregona	laver le sol	wischen (Boden)
to punish	castigar a alguien	punir	bestrafen
to push	empujar a alguien	pousser	schubsen
to scold	reñir a alguien	gronder	ausschimpfen
to set limits	poner límites	imposer des limites	Grenzen setzen
to set the table	poner la mesa	mettre la table	Tisch decken
to shiver	tiritar	frissonner	frösteln
to stroke	acariciar	caresser	streicheln
to struggle	patalear	gigoter	strampeln

English	Spanish	French	German
to sweat	transpirar	transpirer	schwitzen
to take care of	cuidar	surveiller	aufpassen
to teethe	dentar	faire les dents	zahnen
to tickle	cosquillar a alguien	chatouiller	kitzeln
to tinker	hacer tabajos manuales	activités manuelles	basteln
to vomit	vomitar	vomir	erbrechen
tricycle	triciclo (m)	tricycle (m)	Dreirad (n)
washing machine	lavadora (f)	lave (m) linge	Waschmaschine (f)
washing powder	detergente (m)	produit (m) de lessive	Waschmittel (n)
will	voluntad (f)	volonté (f)	Wille (m)
wound	herida (f)	blessure (f)	Wunde (f)

Useful Adresses, Websites and Apps

International Au Pair Association

www.iapa.org

Embassies and Ministry of Foreign Affairs

Australia

www.immi.gov.au

Denmark

www.daenemark.org

Finland

www.formin.finland.fi

France

www.diplomatie.gouv.fr

Germany

www.auswaertiges-amt.de

Great Britain

www.gov.uk/government/organisations/foreign-commonwealth-office

Ireland

www.dfa.ie

Canada

www.international.gc.ca

New Zealand

www.nzembassy.com

Norway

www.regjeringen.no

Sweden

www.government.se

Switzerland

www.eda.admin.ch

Spain

www.maec.es

USA

www.state.gov

Websites

http://www.exchange-rates.org

http://24timezones.com

http://www.weather.com/

http://www.eardex.com

Apps

Au Pair Guide

Travel Guide

Dictionary

Exchange Rate

Weather

News

Insurance

Be an au pair and work & travel safely worldwide

- comprehensive insurance cover
- medical repatriation
- 24-hour emergency assistance
- fast claim processing

Fast & easy online application at www.aupair-insurance-worldwide.com

About the Author

An interest in travel and languages has brought Carmen Kurz to many places and led her to study various cultures. The trained nurse has been a host mother to various au pairs and language students over the past 15 years. This experience makes her intimately familiar with the needs, desires and expectations that au pairs have while also providing her with solid insight into the hopes and fears that parents and host families often have.

In 2008, she founded the educational travel service flyOUT – Foreign Language Youth Agency, which organizes trips abroad for youth, students and young professionals around the world. In 2011, she launched the publishing house flyOUT.

Au Pair
Guide

✈ worldwide

Printed in Great Britain
by Amazon.co.uk, Ltd.,
Marston Gate.